Francis Butler

Breeding, training, management, diseases & c. of dogs

Francis Butler

Breeding, training, management, diseases & c. of dogs

ISBN/EAN: 9783337814861

Printed in Europe, USA, Canada, Australia, Japan

Cover: Foto ©ninafisch / pixelio.de

More available books at **www.hansebooks.com**

BREEDING, TRAINING.

Management, Diseases, &c.

OF

DOGS:

Together with an easy and agreeable Method of Instructing all Breeds of Dogs in a great variety of Amusing and Useful Performances.

INCLUDING THIRTY-ONE ILLUSTRATIONS OF THE DIFFERENT BREEDS OF DOGS, POETICALLY DESCRIBED.

By FRANCIS BUTLER,

AUTHOR OF THE "SPANISH TEACHER," "FRENCH SPEAKER," "DOGS POETICALLY DESCRIBED AND ILLUSTRATED," ETC.

FIFTH EDITION, REVISED AND ENLARGED, WITH AN APPENDIX.

Brooklyn, E. D.

PUBLISHED BY D. S. HOLMES,

89 FOURTH STREET.

INTRODUCTION.

Born a Poet, by instinct a Naturalist, and by profession a Philosopher, I offer no apology in introducing to you a series of Canine poems, descriptive of the varied types of Dogdom; trusting that my delineations may prove both instructive and amusing to the reader, and profitable to the Author,

FRANCIS BUTLER.

PUBLISHER'S NOTICE.

The Publisher trusts, in giving to the public this fifth edition of the work of Francis Butler, deceased, that the additions and embelishments which he has spared neither pains nor expense to procure, will gratify the admirers of the subjects illustrated. Of the late author of the work, it is useless to speak. He has been acknowledged, not only in this country, but in Europe, to be the best American authority on the subject he treats. Mr. Edward Jesse, Keeper of the Queens Park, London, in his "Anecdotes of Dogs," quotes from Mr. Butler's work as the best extant.

WATERFORD

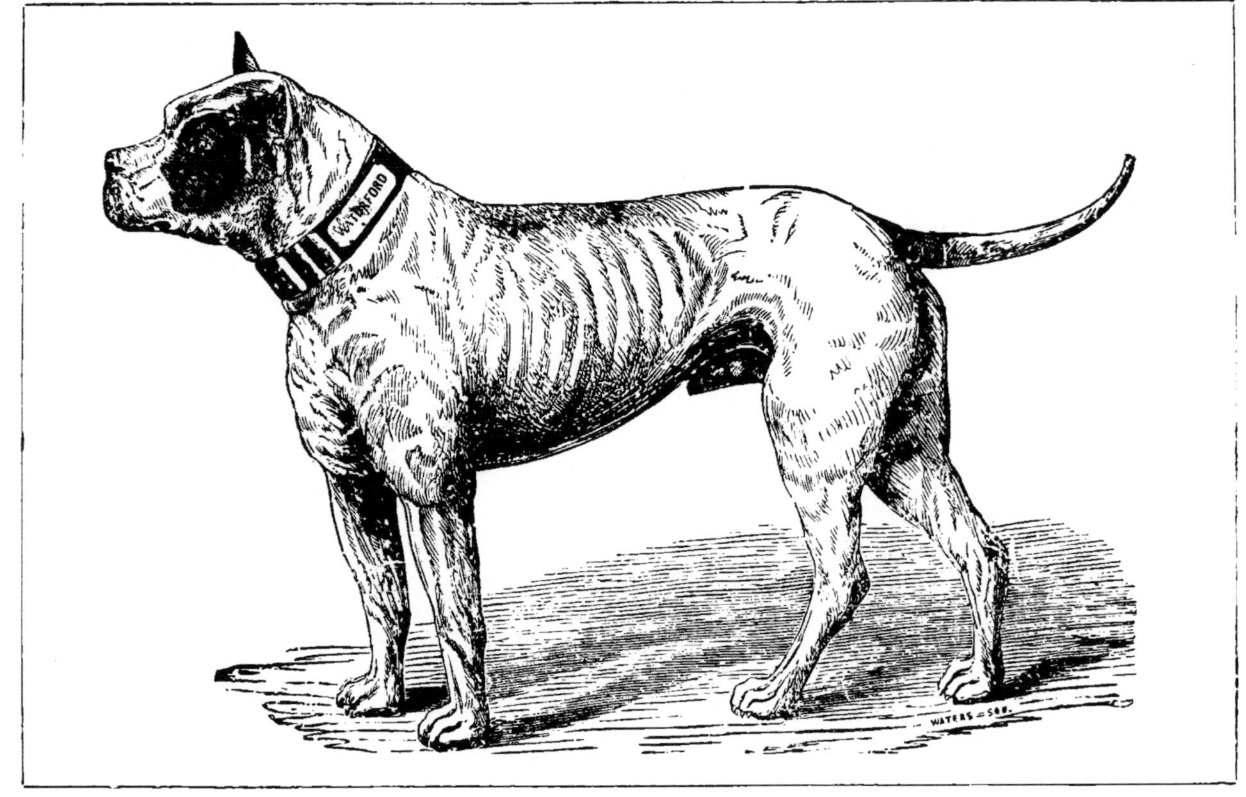
WATERFORD

CONTENTS.

CONTENTS OF APPENDIX.

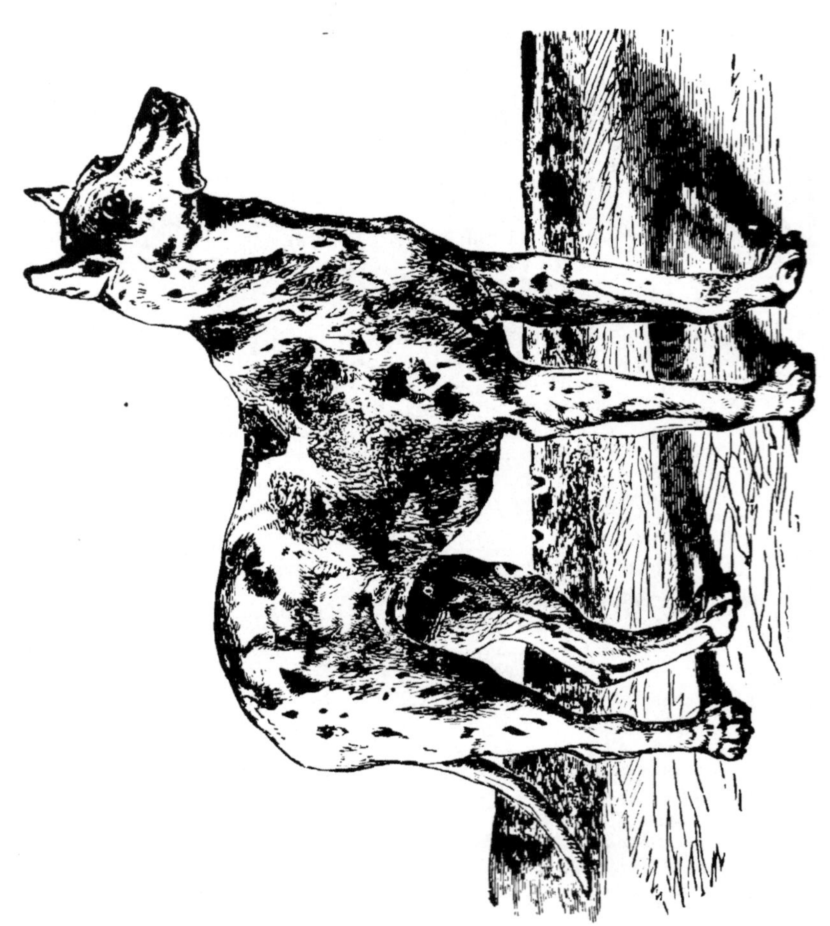

GREAT SIBERIAN BLOODHOUND

GREAT SIBERIAN BLOODHOUND.

Of ancient birth, in form majestic, tall,
And rightly styled by Buffon, king of all;
His strength and prowess dare the wolf and bear,
And fearless taunt the lion in his lair.
In days of yore, in Rome he played his part,
And furnished emblems for the sculptor's art;
His daring feats the chiselled block portrays;
His fame survives, when crumbling stone decays.
When gladiators met in skill to vie,
His noble form was seen expectant by;
In conscious power, the meaner beasts he scorned;
With anxious rage, the rampant tiger warned;
Trained to the fight and eager for the fray,
Dauntless, he rushes on his quiv'ring prey,
The palsied victim struggles all in vain,
The purple flood his polished ivories drain.
Of late alone, has been the fact revealed,
The Ural monatains had his home concealed;
For travellers, oft had fruitless sought to trace
This noble scion, of the canine race.
Now brought to light, his beauteous form we scan,
And wonder when and whence his name began;
While legend, statue, verse, his deeds recall,
Our voices echo "Crown him king of all."

INTRODUCTION.

As Doctors seldom agree, and the wisest Philosophers are occasionally deceived, it would indeed be somewhat surprising, should I, (a non-professional *Dogmatist*, possessing a very imperfect knowledge of anatomy and chemistry), at least draw some crooked inferences, both from standard facts and from the results of my own personal experience. We are all more or less liable to error; but whilst the false conclusions of Philosophers are handed down to us as incontrovertible truths, none daring to contradict, I humbly request my readers to credit nothing from my pen, that may be in anywise revolting to their reason and common sense. Great men can write what they please, and it were the height of presumption to doubt the soundness of their arguments, or question the correctness of their conclusions.

Buffon, (the celebrated French Naturalist),

readily accounts for the lack of hair on the Turkish dog, by presuming the stock to have become degenerated by Mange or some other cutaneous disease, thus bequeathing bare pelts and scabby hides to all their future generations. This same Baffon also states that the Shepherd-dog is the origin of the whole canine fraternity. Now I dare doubt the proof of either of these assertions: of the former, because, if a cutaneous disease were the cause of the absence of hair on the Turkish and other dogs. they would be the visible subjects of the contagion, whilst not only their hides, but their constitutions would be the sufferers; whereas, they are less subject to Mange than the heavier clad. In the second place, what ground can there be for supposing that the Bull-dog, Greyhound, &c., are direct lineal descendants of the Shepherd-dog, when there is as much difference even in the varied breeds of Shepherd-dogs, as between the Newfoundland and Pug! But these conclusions are considered as undeniable facts. Why? because the great Buffon says so.

Youatt, an esteemed author on canine pathology, remarks: "It is singular that the Greyhound exhibits so little power of scent; but this is simply because he has never been taught to use it, or has been cruelly corrected, when he has attempted to exercise it." If this be fair reasoning, it might also appear logical to infer, that the offspring of animals, who had been broken from eating meat, or barking at night, would naturally inherit the particular teachings of their forefathers. I am willing to admit that talents to a certain extent may be hereditary, but the sudden annihilation of an instinct I could never believe, before I had raised a litter or two of three-legged puppies, from a slut who had unfortunately lost a limb.

The same author also states that it is only in England that the Shepherd-dog injures and worries the sheep. I can account for this assertion in no other way, than by supposing that the writer of it had not yet crossed the Channel, or he might have returned with the impression that Paris Poodles all learn to dance. He also appears to take it for granted, that the relative weight of the brain is an unerring criterion of intellectual power; and *to illustrate his theory*, he adds, that the brain of a man is a thirtieth of his entire weight, that of the Newfoundland, a sixtieth; of the Poodle, a hundreth; and of the *ferocious and stupid Bull-dog*, only a three hundredth part of its entire weight. This may be true, but, as it does not tally with my experience on the subject of canine phrenology, I cannot corroborate such a conclusion: for instance, it would be difficult to prove to me, that the offspring of a cross between the Bull-dog and Newfoundland would only have half the sense of a Newfound land, pure, any more than I can believe that the Newfoundland has two-fifths more of intellect than the Poodle. Besides, I have made many researches among canine skulls, and am rather inclined to award the premium of merit to quality than to quantity. Pliny, the great Historian. states that the King of Albania made Alexander a present of a Dog, to which the latter introduced wild Boars and Bears. Of these the Dog took no notice, upon which Alexander ordered him to be killed for his cowardice. When the King of Albania hears of this, he sends Alexander another Dog, telling him he should not make a trial with such *insignificant animals*, but rather with a Lion or an Elephant. Alexander being much surprised, (*and well he might!*) made immediate preparation for a trial, and soon saw the Lion prostrate, with his back broken. Then the Elephant was produced. The Dog maintained such an ingenious combat with the Elephant, that the latter ultimately came down with a crash, that made the earth tremble with the fall. In reference to this, Youatt says, that possibly the English Bull-dog is the same breed. Only imagine, gent'e reader, an English Bull-dog breaking a Lion's back, and overcoming an Elephant in single combat. Now the largest English Mastiffs have been loosened on the Lion in successive pairs, and were annihilated in a twinkling. Pliny's Dog then must indeed have been a *Rouser!* The effects of climate are now easily accounted for! What would Buffon's *original* Shepherd-dog have thought, had he witnessed the strength and prowess of his dauntless descendant?

I do not quote these remarkable sayings of wonderful men, either as a critic or a fault finder, but to plead for mercy in advance in behalf of my unworthy self, should I, perchance, be accused of similar misapprehensions. I trust, however, that by carefully keeping within the limits of my range, and avoiding the unfathomable depths of metaphysical suppositions, I may somewhat elucidate and simplify the mystified art of Dog-management, presenting simple facts, free from incomprehensible technicalities, and in such a light, that they may be understood, and freely digested by the *non-professional*.

THE DOG.

THE DOG appears to be a native of every cli mate: in the frigid regions of the North, under the burning sun of the Tropics, or in the more temperate climes, he is to be found the faithful associate, guardian and friend of man; whilst, if we are to believe what everybody says, the most sagacious, knowing, tractable, learned and faithful, are common in every part of the habitable globe. From the mammoth St. Bernard, down to the darling, dear, tiny, little lap-dog, no matter what breed, what cross, what size, what color, or what his peculiar properties or propensities, the favorite is considered by his owner, as knowing far more than the majority of other breeds. The St. Bernard has rendered himself famous, by his charitable feats in relieving snow-bound travellers; the Newfound land by saving human beings from drowning; the Poodle by his aptness in acquiring a host of amusing tricks and antics; the Sporting Dog, by his services in the field, contributing both to the pleasure and profit of his master; the pet, (whatever may be his pedigree), for his almost incredible foresight, judgment, discretion, attention, cleanliness, &c., in fine, to hear some people speak of their pets, one might be led to believe their dogs learned enough to instruct the whole family. I am only endeavoring to show by this, that the society of man, together with education and the force of habit, produce about the same effects on one breed as on the other. I am often asked which kind is the most easy to teach, and I am certainly unable to give any satisfactory answer. Whilst almost every breed of dog has its peculiar characteristics, and is more apt at one branch of tuition than another, still, as a whole, I can scarcely admit that the honorable member from Newfoundland, or the noble representative of St. Bernard, is more capable of instruction than the learned Poodle from Paris, or the thirsty Bloodhound of Cuba. By habits, education, good society and good management, they will all excel in their varied spheres, and will all be considered, (as no doubt they are), the most wonderful animals in the world. A large handsome dog, or an elegant pet, is generally observed to be the most tractable, and gentlemanly animal. He receives a lesson at every step, his master or mistress is proud of him, he accompanies them around the house, and ofttimes in their travels; he must be introduced to a large circle of acquaintances, who are called on to witness his performances, and testify to his merit. The pretty, little dog, in the house knows the varied habits and movements of the inmates, the hour to rise, and the hour of retirement; breakfast, dinner and tea are seasons with which he is perfectly familiar; in fact, he appears to understand a hundred things he never was taught; whilst the poor beast of a watch-dog, at the end of his four foot chain, is justly accused of being one of the most untractable, illiterate brutes in creation. Society, habit and example are the sole causes of this difference. Had the pet been on the chain, and the forlorn watch-dog inside, the reverse would have been the case.

Some date the origin of the Dog to the Wolf, but as there is a wide difference both in their physical construction and intellectual capabilities, there is no foundation for such an insupportable theory. No · a dog is a dog, always has been, and ever will be. He differs widely in many respects from any other quadruped, surpassing them all in sagacity, intellectuality and fidelity. The elephant, the horse, the cow, the monkey, and others may portray evident symptoms of instinctive reasoning, but the dog will absorb more instruction in one short hour, than the whole phalanx could digest in a week. He will learn where no lesson is given, and from knowledge thus acquired, he is fully competent to act as the tutor of others. With his wonderful performances, and disinterested fidelity, the whole world appear to be conversant. A recapitulation of his varied feats would be a somewhat useless devotion of space, whilst to pass them over in utter silence, would be unjust in one, who is proud to acknowledge him his trustworthy friend. In various parts of the world, I have traced the peculiar characteristics of the canine race, and have found that they stand everywhere pre-eminent

ST. BERNARD

SAINT BERNARD DOG.

Of tawny color, and of lion size,
In muscle powerful, and by instinct wise,
On his bold front, there lurks no treach'rous
grin,
Candor without, and honesty within;
The trusty Guardian of the holy friar,
Sleepless, he dozes, by the convent fire;
But roused to action, braves the frost and snow,
To greet a friend, or face a daring foe.
On barren peaks, abstemious monks grow fat,
Feasting on strangers' charity at that;
Without a friend, e'en to a saint 't were hard,
To brave the rigors of the bleak Bernard.
From this huge mount, the Dog derives his name;
Some doubt his pedigree, but none his fame:
For strangers oft, when ice bedecks the ground,
No friend to help in that drear region round;
With hunger perishing, and limbs congealed,
To the chill grasp of death prepare to yield:
When lo! he comes! the gallant Bruno hies!
With food and cordial, e'er the traveller dies.
Some may exclaim, "Can there a man be found,
Who'd dream of bartering such a priceless
hound?"
But then again, Lives there a monk so rash,
To lose a customer, who hands the cash?

above all other animals in their astonishing powers of mental development—their disinterested fidelity and attachment to man. Under chastisement, neglect and starvation, they are still devoted to their master's will, and ready to perish by his side, rather than forsake him; his companion by day, and his guard by night; the author of his sports, the sharer of his toils, and ever in waiting to obey his commands. With all these qualifications, it must not be forgotten, that great talents either uncultivated or misdirected, may be, and often are, turned to very bad account. For this simple reason, "*Dog*" is a bye-word among all nations, because, travel where you may, thousands of these poor brutes are either left to the tender mercies of unrestricted loaferdom, (consequently they are accused of transgressing laws which they were never taught to obey), or even with respectable owners in the majority of cases, they get no kind of instruction whatever; it being generally considered an all sufficient virtue, should they happily succeed in waking up the family, two or three times in the night. If a dog should, however, chance to break loose, kill a dozen chickens, four ducks and a sheep, steal half a leg of mutton, and worry the cat, tear up the flower-beds, or play havoc with the clothes-line, ten to one but the general opinion is, that he ought to be shot or got rid of immediately. Now I contend that he has done no more than might have been expected, even from an uncivilized biped. It was nothing more than a perfectly natural impulse unrestrained. If we show a rat to a terrier, and he refuse to seize him, we set him down as a cowardly beast ; but we can either urge him to kill him, or teach him to respect him. He may not require excitement, but at any rate, he may be easily restrained. The greatest rat killer I ever owned, or ever saw, was my Bull-terrier dog Tiger, (whose Life and Adventures, lately published, may be worth the perusal of all admirers of canine character). I could leave him in a room shut up with half a dozen rats, running around him, and had I told him not to touch them, they were perfectly safe in his keeping ; but at a word, and in a few seconds he would annihilate them all. Were he ever so hungry, he would hold meat in his mouth, till I bid him swallow it ; he would obey a multitude of commands, given in a whisper ; yea, a variety of so called remarkable things could old Tiger do. Now, I am not aware that he was born with talents superior to his fellows, neither did he belong to a race the most renowned for their intellectuality, but he had his advantages. He was seldom out of my sight or hearing, and his progress afforded us mutual pleasure and satisfaction. During the seventeen years of his life, I seldom had any occasion to correct him with stripes; he knew the expression of my countenance, and the sound of my voice too well to require it. So accustomed was I to the different intonations of his bark, that to me, it was nothing short of absolute speech. I repeat, I do not quote him as being naturally more gifted than his fellows, (although there is an equally marked difference of capacity in dogs as well as in men), since I have had many who profited equally, according to their advantages. I merely introduce his respected memory, to prove to a demonstration that dogs are really worthy of respectful consideration, and will amply repay any reasonable trouble that may be bestowed on them; whilst on the other hand, he who would deny his guardian the privilege of a common school education, should be called to account for his short-sighted, and cruel neglect.

NEWFOUNDLAND.

NEWFOUNDLAND DOG.

Of glossy black, in form and bearing grand,
The noted Fisher-dog of Newfoundland;
Water his element, the sea his rest,
Of all amphibious, surely he's the best.
Massive in limb, his organs well defined,
His shaggy coat defies the stormy wind;
With dauntless foot, he stems the ocean spray,
Nor foaming surge can check his onward way.
From North to South, a household word his name,
While East and West, re echo loud his fame;
His truthful looks with confidence inspire
The cradled infant and the aged Sire.
'T were vain, in verse, his merits to relate;
A task, his virtues to exaggerate;
Playmate by day, and sentinel by night,
The parents' guardian, and the boys' delight.
The tempest rages, and the sea grows wild,
The mother screams, "Who'll save my drowning child?"
The gallant Neptune dashes from the shore,
And rescues him who sank to rise no more.
The house in flames, or burglars breaking through;
He'll guard your purse, and rouse you quickly too;
In joy and sorrow, he's your trusty friend,
Honest and faithful, bribeless, to the end.

ORIGIN OF THE DIFFERENT BREEDS OF DOGS.

This is rather a hard subject for a discourse; such is the diversity of opinion, in regard to the prime origin of the different shades of Dogdom. There being nothing more than an almost imaginary circumstantial train of doubtful evidence, to substantiate a variety of suppositions, we are left somewhat in the dark as to the peculiar varieties of the parent stock. From a lengthened experience in obtaining crosses of different breeds, and from a thousand instances I have witnessed of the varied products of untraceable mongrel stock; from the incredible changes which climate affects even on the same generation, I am inclined to believe that many breeds, now considered as genuine, might be again reproduced from opposite races. I believe this, because I have often proved it

There are, however, some races which bear more the impress of originality than others, both in their outward appearance, and in their instinctive propensities. The courage of the Bull-dog; the fleetness and sight of the Greyhound; the game hunting attitudes of the Pointer; the long curly ears of the Spaniel; the peculiar drooping ears of the Hound. These and other examples of peculiarities of physical structure, and native properties, lead us to infer an originality of caste. But from these few only, which I have mentioned, what an infinite variety may be propagated! The Hound with a Spaniel, and the offspring crossed by a Pointer would certainly be running great risk of producing a Setter. The Setter thus formed, crossed by a Bull-dog, might turn out some tolerable fair Terriers. Thus, by the blending of different stamps of animals, there is scarcely any limit to strange productions. Add to this, the effects of habit, diet and climate, and it is easily conceived how every generation is introduced to a novel canine race, of which our ancestors had never dreamed. An animal not only changes his appearance to suit the climate he may be called on to inhabit, but moreover, his very instincts are forced into that particular channel, best adapted to the life he has to lead. Like man himself, he is in a great measure the creature of circumstances, and his peculiar attributes and acquirements are to a certain extent hereditary, as well as his snub nose, curly ears, or spindle shanks. The effects of climate on animals are really astonishing. Witness only the Merino sheep in Cuba; the Norman horse in London; compare the fur of the fox or rabbit in different latitudes, and you will be convinced what a variety of changes may be thus produced on the animal system. This, together with the constant introduction of new stock into almost every country, will account in a great measure for the numerous varieties and sub-varieties of the canine species. The breeds best known and most in use in this country, are the Pointer, Setter, Spaniel, Fox-hound, Beagle, Greyhound, Bull-dog, Bull-terrier, Scotch and English Terrier, Newfoundland, St. Bernard, Scotch and English Shepherd-dog, Poodle, &c. From these alone, only imagine what an endless transmogrification might be effected! Some of these make good cross breeds, particularly the

St. Bernard and Newfoundland. This amalgamation adds to the beauty of the St. Bernard, and to the size of the Newfoundland; and, I think is the happiest mixture for an imposing and trustworthy family watch dog. Nevertheless, as this is the only cross I care about, I shall not enlarge on the subject; in other cases I prefer the pure stock, as far as it can be depended on, unless a cross be persisted in, until it turns out to suit one's purpose. Nevertheless, a little Hound in the Pointer, a little Spaniel in the Setter, &c., if judgmatically infused, may serve to arouse the dormant energies of an out-bred stock, and impart new vigor to a novel procreation. In fact, no breed can be sustained, without an occasional sprinkle of foreign blood, except, at the risk of sacrificing health and strength, and of eventually dwindling our chosen ones to perfect nonentities—weak, puny, lifeless, worthless.

THE BLOODHOUND.

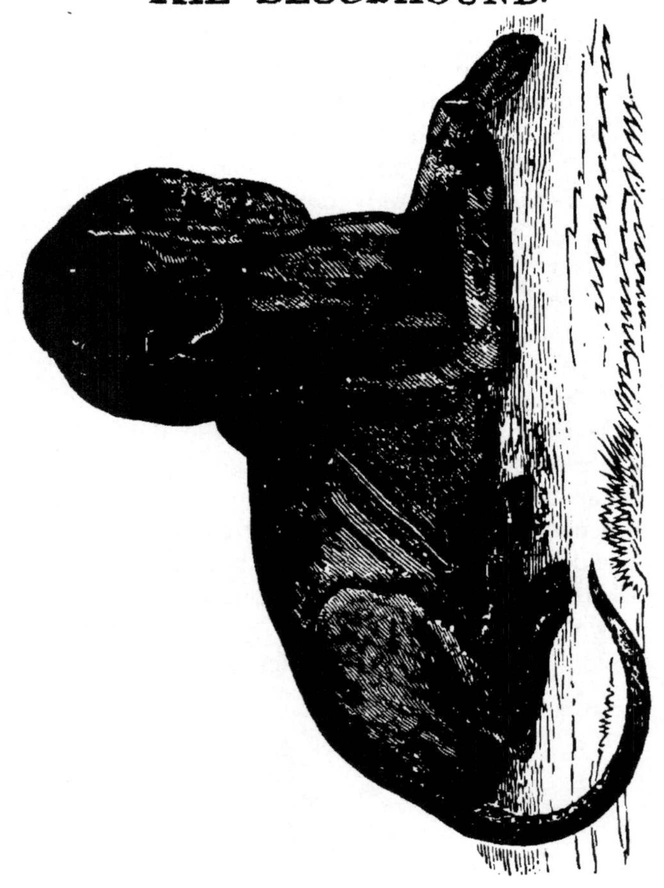

THE BLOODHOUND.

Dreaded his name, for bloody deeds renowned,
Once in old England, now in Cuba found.
Ears broad and pendant, heavy drooping jowi;
Fearful his bark, and ominous his howl.
Of color tawny, or of reddish tan,
Sometimes the friend, yet oft' a foe to man;
Of nervous limb, with teeth deep set and long,
Disputes the mastery of the canine throng.
The thief's antipathy, the murderer's dread,
He tracks their pathway, notes their every tread;
On tireless foot and panting for the fight,
Trails the doomed fugitive, by day and night.
And men there are, who hire him by the day,
To hunt the trembling Negro-runaway; [flood,
Nor wood. nor swamp, nor brake, nor bursting
Can daunt his ardent rage, for human blood;
Onward he speeds, low scenting on the ground,
With deep and sonorous yell at every bound;
The race is o'er, the Bloodhound wins the day,
His wreaking jaws in triumph seize the prey.
His name a bye-word " A ferocious brute."
His vice constrained, inhuman brutes to suit.
For thirsty blood ounds, if but rightly mann'd,
Are kind and docile as the Newfoundland.

To prove my doctrine, I would here assert,
That virtue's often vice if kept inert,
That vice is virtue, when in duty found,
For who would prize a disobedient hound!

BREEDING OF DOGS.

It is an old saying, and a true one: "Nothing like a good beginning." This proverb stands particularly *staunch* with regard to dogs. Without a sound start, we shall be often subject to sore disappointments. When we consider the unsuitable amalgamations; the interminable, and almost incomprehensible transmogrifications; the oft trebly compounded admixtures, to which the canine race is continually exposed, it should inspire us with somewhat of diffidence, in attempting to define the originality of stock, or in deciding on the purity of blood, simply from outward appearances. Breeds of dogs are continually undergoing the varied changes of the kaleidoscope. When there may chance to be nine shades on the one side, and perhaps, thirteen on the other, it would be preposterous to inquire under what head to class the progeny. Certainly, they would be commonly termed mongrels; but not more than three breeds at most, could be detected in their appearance; whilst their peculiar characteristics could be named only after trial. It often happens, however, even from such an inscrutable compound as that above mentioned, that a dog of apparently pure stock may present himself. Hence we are often deceived. We get Pointers, that won't hunt; Water Spaniels, that won't face the water; Newfoundlands intractable and savage; Bull-dogs that won't fight; Charley Spaniels with long noses; Terriers with round heads; in fine, a multitude of animals with irresponsible hypocritical countenances, well calculated to subvert the judgment of a Buffon, a Cuvier, or of *Butler himself*.

I merely cite these examples, to show how careful we ought to be in the selection of Breeding-Stock. I have seen splendid Scotch Terriers from a Poodle; magnificent Newfoundlands from a Foxhound; beautiful Black and Tan Terriers from a Cocker Spaniel; also three apparently distinct breeds in the same litter; and a host of almost incredible productions, too numerous to put in print. A peculiar breed will often leak out, from generations back, thus giving rise to the popular, yet mistaken notion, of a slut enclosing in her womb the offspring of various sires. This idea is not only against the laws of nature, but contrary to common sense and experience. One plain fact, (it appears to me), is sufficient to decide the question. A slut will be in full heat during 10 or 20 days. Let us suppose then, that during that period, she has had intercourse with one or more males every day; if her whelps were fathered by a variety of dogs, it is reasonable to suppose, (presuming them to arrive at the regular stage of embryo-perfection), that they would enter the world at periods, corresponding to the various times, when they were begotten; therefore a slut, (one of the random kind), would be from 10 to 20 days in bringing forth her young, which I have hitherto not found to be the case. I have a record of some five or six hundred breeding sluts; sixty hours has been the greatest variation of time. between copulation and parturition. Some, I have put to the same dog every day, from the first up to the twentieth day. Now, why did'nt they pup at various periods? They were as likely to do it from one dog, as from a hundred; but they have not averaged between the first born puppy and the last, perhaps over twelve hours. Then again, those who have for several consecutive days been subjected to the embraces of Pointer, Poodle and Pug, are just as regular in bringing forth, as others who have been allowed one male alone. The difference often discernable in the same family of *pure breeds*, arises from some former and perhaps distant ama'gamation of another race. In breeding then, I repeat be very cautious in the selection of your stock. Trace their pedigree, (if you can), their qualities and their characteristics; aye, their manners and education; their constitutions, pluck, endurance, &c. I cannot rid myself of the idea that even talents and acquirements are somewhat hereditary. The quail trembles at the tread of man, and with the very shell on his back, hurries off affrighted at the sound of his footstep; whilst the young turkey, or chicken, (once wild as the quail), will become friendly in a few minutes; and in a few hours will follow a person about as his adopted parent. The steady habits of the parent stock have thoroughly transformed their instinctive endowments, and suited them to civilized life. Look at the tame rabbit, (a more apt illustration), the young ones are comparatively tame, when they first run about; whilst those of the same stamp, if born in the woods, at the least sound, would bolt off like a shot, from under the very mother that bore them. Do not suppose, however, that you can get a learned puppy; neither can absolute confidence be placed in hereditary endowments. I quote these examples merely to endeavor to substantiate my impressions in regard to the superiority of educated stock.

The next point to be considered is, the absolute Breeding. Authors are continually at variance as to the most appropriate ages for propagation. My own personal experience has not led me to fix on any definite period of canine development, as more particularly suitable for procreation, except in as far as health nd vigor are concerned. If the dog and slut be perfectly healthy, and fully developed; if they have lost none of their vigor; if they be free from all taint of hereditary disease, stock may be safely relied on, from animals varying in age from eighteen months, to eight years; and occasionally older. It is commonly supposed that the first litter is not good for much. I admit, there are cases, when the slut is in heat, before completing her growth, the pups would not, perhaps, be as fine; but as a general rule, Nature is the best indicator of procreative fitness. This, I really do believe, that dogs bred from very young, uneducated stock, are much wilder and more difficult to control, than the offspring of riper years. See that your breeders are symmetrically built; strong in the loins, good teeth, good coat, and well developed limbs. Reject contracted chests, narrow loins, decayed teeth, stinking breath, &c. Do not *breed in*, any more than can be avoided; it tells unhappy tales, and if persisted in, to any extent, deteriorates the constitution, weakens the intellectual powers, and gradually extinguishes every spark of healthful vigor. If you are particular about breeding from the same stock, that dog should be chosen who is living at the greatest distance from his mate. This will make an astonishing difference, as climate, diet, habits and treatment contribute greatly towards a physical change. Witness the same breed of dog, horse, cow, sheep, &c., under different suns. If these causes work such a marked change, the principle must be carried out in the same ratio, in localities less distant, and climates less varying.

MR. JOHN E. T. GRAINGER'S SETTER "NELLY" AND HER PUPS, VALUED AT $5,000.

SLUTS IN HEAT. PUPPING AND PUPS.

One of the most important things in Breeding is, the absolute certainty that the female has not been tainted by forbidden suitors. Great caution is necessary during the copulative period, as both male and female are equally desirous of satisfying their lust at whatever risk. The slut then should be kept where no dog, (except the chosen one), can possibly have access. Of this, the owner himself should be absolutely certain, as hirelings are often ignorant and generally careless about the necessary precautions. The general idea is that the heated period is of nine days duration; but this is by no means certain, as it differs widely in different subjects, varying from three sometimes to twenty days; perhaps the average may be nine or ten days. The female generally indicates its approach by a gradual expansion

SCOTCH DEERHOUND.

SCOTCH DEERHOUND.

Full many a bard, his glorious feats has sung;
Full many a hall, his echoed praises rung;
Where trophied antlers o'er the feast preside,
Bold Oscar couching by famed Lufra's side.
Most noble hound! of Scotia's lairds the boast!
And highly prized on Albion's sportive coast!
His brawny limb and wiry coat outvie
The classic greyhound and the roughy Skye.
In stature tall, imposing gait and mien,
Near festive boards of Royalty is seen;
Bright piercing ken and scrutinizing eye,
Cool, dauntless courage, that none dare defy;
His eagle glance, the distant game reviews,
With lightning speed, the bounding stag pursues;
With bursting ardor, void of every fear,
Impetuous rushes on the fated deer.
O'er rock and chasm, he darts, the daring hound,
Nor ought arrests his bold and reckless bound;
With fatal grasp, retains the destined prey,
Tho' mortal wounds his prowess oft' repay.
Mark well his joy, as home the prize they bear,
His martial step, his proud victorious air;
By speaking gesture, glories in his name,
And eyes exultingly the lifeless game.

of the generative organs, from which, (previous to her being prepared for the male) is observed to issue a bloody fluid, more particularly visible after her having lain still for a time. These preparatory symptoms are of more or less duration, in different subjects. I have known them to continue a month previous to a perfect development, and even then all communication with the male refused. Very rarely will the slut submit to the dog, till this has passed off; indeed it is not fit she should, as the organs are not yet thoroughly conditioned for copulation, and a favorable result cannot be anticipated. The female should, more properly, be put to the male three or four days after she has ceased to bleed, as, at the outset, the womb is apt either to reject, or is unprepared to cherish the seed; consequently early amalgamations often prove fruitless. Should she continue in heat, for several days, after having taken the male, it will be advisable to have the operation renewed, as the protracted expansive longing of the parts is apt to allow the evacuation of the semen. The female may be impregnated the first, second or third time, &c., it is impossible (before pupping) to say which. It is also, impossible to know, for an absolute fact, (but experience has caused me to believe from incontrovertible circumstantial evidence), that what has been done, may be undone. For instance, should you put your slut to a dog, (who is considered an excellent stock-getter), and she should happen four or five days after to come in contact with another male, it will very often happen that the second is the father of the anticipated family. This of course, is proved by the day of the pupping. For this reason, I am not an advocate of oft-repeated doses ; for, granting that it can be undone, it may be undone without being replaced. Once may be equal to a dozen times, provided both be in a prepared and healthy state. I generally advise twice, missing two days between the operations ; especially, when we are not satisfied as to the time the female has been in full heat. Whilst I do not depend on it too early, I often fear lest it may be too late. It is not well to shut up the animals together, when it can be otherwise effected ; the male is apt to wear himself out uselessly, which diminishes, rather than adds to the prospect of an increase. In case of necessity, when there is a difference in height of the two animals, a square board of sufficient size, may be used with two holes cut in it, to admit the legs of the slut (should she be the tallest ;) or for her to stand on, should she be the lowest. It may be raised to any height by placing something for the edges to bear on. Sluts intended for breeding should not be kept too fat, neither when bearing ; in the first place, they are very apt to miss ; and in the second, to experience great difficulty and danger in bringing forth. Dogs too fat are also very indifferent and uncertain stock-getters. During pregnancy, grossness and excess of food should be particularly guarded against ; especially with the more delicate breeds ; at the same time the animal should by no means be kept low. Food that is too strong for puppies is (in delicate constitutions), too strong for bearing-sluts. The mother is apt to get too fat and humory ; consequently, the brood is with difficulty brought into the world, and the life of both mother and offspring is jeopardised ; secondly, the pups are often born full of eruptions, and more subject to disease. House-pets, when in this state, should not be allowed to go up and down stairs ; especially after the sixth week

Numbers of litters are in this way weakened or destroyed, and numerous mothers sacrificed. It appears to me, to be an unnatural canine movement, this ascending and descending of steps, and I imagine, (with sluts in whelp), it strains the sustaining ligament, through which the nourishment passes to the embryos ; thus proving decidedly injurious both to mother and offspring. Regular exercise should always be attended to, and need not be seriously diminished on account of pregnancy. Sporting dogs, however, should not be hunted much when far advanced, as they are subject to sudden jerks, which might prove injurious. A snug, comfortable place should be selected, and a warm bed should be prepared for the slut, to deposit her pups. She should be accustomed to it, for several days previous to her delivery. This generally has the effect of confining her labors to one spot ; otherwise she is apt, in her pains, to drop them about at random, thus unnecessarily perilling their lives. Should she absolutely appear determined on the selection of another spot, it is better to humor her, and there make her as comfortable as possible. A peeping, meddling curiosity at the time of pupping should not be allowed; she is generally far better alone, since inquisitiveness will sometimes cause the animal to injure or even destroy her young, in endeavoring to conceal them. Should she however show symptoms of lengthened labor, small doses of castor oil may be administered every half hour, until an operation or a delivery be secured. Should a surgical operation appear to be necessary, you had better run the risk of doing nothing, than to meddle with what you do not understand. In such a case, apply to any, who may have had some experience, to help you out of the predicament. Many things have been recommended, to facilitate labor, but not being satisfied of their safety and efficacy, I shall not introduce them here. I have never lost a single slut in labor yet, and have used no other means and precautions than those here mentioned; I am therefore satisfied with my own treatment. The object of this work is not to repeat what others say, but to state what (I believe) I know myself. That thousands will differ from me, as I take the liberty of doing from them, I have not the least shadow of a doubt, still I remain convinced that a bushel of experience is worth a whole chaldron of hearsay.

Soon after pupping, warm drinks are both soothing and beneficial, such as warm milk, broth or gruel or any light, warm emollient, the patient may relish. But, it is not necessary to enforce it, or to disturb the family to insist on it; a little may be presented in a tea cup; if she partake of it, more may be given. The pups should be as little handled as possible; it distresses them to bear on their bowels, and the constant habit of handling them should be avoided, more particularly in delicate breeds. If the slut should have an abundant supply of milk, the pups will not want feeding, before they are five weeks old; in fact, they are better without it. Should the mother be a poor milker, they may be helped along by warm milk and water, (half and half) light broths and such like, which they may be taught to lap as early as the third week, or they may be raised from a bottle, in the same way as a child, even from their birth. The main difficulty in raising them by hand, is in keeping them perfectly dry, warm and clean. With all possible attention, there is nothing like a mother's care; nevertheless, they generally get along very well, by your strictly attending to the above. Keeping many with the mother too long, retards rather than promotes their growth, as they do not feed as freely, while depending on the mother; at the same time, perhaps, she may not be able to supply half their demands. One pup left with the slut generally out-thrives the rest, upon the principle that what will starve a family will fatten one. He will also, be generally more forward in his antics, from having been under his mother's undivided attention. The mother's snapping and pinching her pups is no proof of her wishing to get rid of them altogether. She will invariably allow them to suck, when she has any amount of milk for them, but as they would drag her to death, if they had their own way, she is compelled to repulse them in her own defense, and make them wait her own time. After the fourth week or sometimes earlier, it is cruel to force the slut to remain the whole time with them, as they are a source of constant annoyance to her. When this is the case, it is better to keep her from them, except at noon-time and during the night. I consider the most critical period for pups, to be between the age of two and four months. Bad food, lack of a comfortable bed, damp feet or too much exposure, at this tender age are apt to bring on Distemper, Inflammation of the lungs or bowels, often terminating in hasty consumption. Nevertheless, a delicate bred pup should not be brought up too tenderly; the object should be carefully to harden the constitution by degrees, according to the best judgment of the owner.

Suitable food, air, and exercise are as essential to the health of the dog as to that of his master. This being attended to, he will seldom require either pill, powder or draft.

The best food for puppies is a well boiled mixture of meat and meal. *Viz*: Sheep's heads boiled to a rag, the bones all carefully removed, and the meat chopped fine and replaced in the boiler, then add about the same bulk of Indian meal; boil them well together about ten minutes, stirring all the time. Turn it out and you have a fine pudding to be fed at discretion. A little salt should always be added when boiling. The proportion of meal may be a little increased, when the meat is more nutritive. Avoid Pork and all salted meats, and

FOX HOUND.

FOX HOUND.

The prince of hunters, dashing, bold and free,
The master hound, of sportive pedigree.
About the size of Pointer, more or less,
Tho' stouter built and differing some in dress;
Less fine in coat, in limb more stubborn grown,
A Pointer's tail a Foxhound would disown.
His graceful ear and eye of daring mood,
Distinctive preface to unsullied blood.
To English Staghound near akin may be,
Yet lighter made, a fleeter hound than he;
Seldom or ever of one color bred,
Black and tan; red, white; black, white and red.
The glories of hunting ye ne'er would deny,
Did ye once see a pack of such dogs in full cry;
Mark Jollyboy, Chanticleer leading the chase;
See Barmaid and Faraway quicken their pace;
Note Dewdrop and Forrester hard on the track;
With old Ringwood, heading the rest of the
pack.
Hark! hark to their voices, so mellow and clear,
As the brush of poor Renard, they eagerly near;
On, on dash the huntsmen in scarlet and white,
With their high mettled steeds, in ecstatic de-
light;
Hear! hear the glad echos, that merrily fall
O'er the soul-stirring feast, at the banqueting
hall.

don't let the puppies wet themselves or lie in a damp or dirty bed. Look at them often and see that they are kept free from fleas, lice, dandruff, &c.

MANAGEMENT AND TREATMENT OF DOGS.

It is more important to understand the management of a dog, than to be possessed of a thousand nominal remedies for the cure of his various ailments; inasmuch as the Antidote is at all times preferable to the Cure.

I shall first throw out a few hints on the guardianship of pets. Whilst many are sacrificed, for lack of necessary attendance, there are thousands, who perish prematurely from over doses of kindness. Delicate breeds of Dogs certainly require great care and attention in rearing, but overstrained tenderness is often more dangerous than culpable neglect. The dear little creature, that is allowed to lay under the stove, that is stuffed with delicacies two or three times a day, that is never allowed to breathe the fresh air, except under a cloudless sky, is more subject to colds, fits, rheumatism, sore eyes and ears, worms, &c., than the worthless mongrel, who was raised on the street, neglected and despised. The former are affected by every change of the atmosphere, and subjected to a variety of diseases, unknown to him, who has been hardened from his birth. I ask you then, neither to stuff nor starve; neither to chill nor burn. A house pet should always have a sleeping-place allotted to him, warm and comfortable, not near the fire, nor in the damp. Anything round is better for an animal to lay in; such as a tastefully ornamented cheese-box, or anything of a similar shape. In cold weather, it should not be larger than to contain him comfortably. It is better for the following reasons: he may keep himself perfectly warm, and his bed may be made exactly to fit him; it also takes up less available space than any other shape. He should never be fed to the full, neither excited to eat, when he appears disinclined. Lack of appetite, so common to pampered favorites, is generally the result of an over loaded stomach and disordered digestion. This is easily cured by medicine, but more safely and simply without it. Fast him for twenty-four hours; after which, keep him on half his ordinary allowance; if it agree with him, and he keep in fair condition, continue the regimen. Nursing in the lap is injurious; not in itself, but the animal is thereby subjected to constant chills, in emerging from a snoozy warmth to a cold carpet or chilly bed. A dog accustomed to the lap is always shivering after it. and renders himself quite troublesome by his importunate addresses. A moderate share of nursing is well enough, but should be indulged in only as an occasional treat. Great care should be taken in the washing of delicate dogs. When this operation is performed, they should be rubbed perfectly dry; after which they should be covered. and remain so, till the shivering has completely subsided. The water should be only blood-warm; it is far better than hot, and not so likely to give the animal cold. Injudicious washing and bad drying are productive of running sore eyes, more especially visible in white Poodles, where the hair is long and wooly, retaining the moisture. Once a fortnight is often enough to wash any dog but a white one. Washing has very little effect in the destruction of Vermin. Fleas can live some time under water, which I have often thought only makes them bite the harder and stick the closer, when reanimated from their temporary torpidity. If "Butler's Mange Liniment and Flea Exterminator" cannot be obtained, the animal may be well sodden with soft soap and washed about ten minutes after. This cannot be done with safety, except in warm weather, In cold weather, the comb may be used, immediately after the application of the soap, as the fleas will then be too stupid to effect their escape. "Butler's Liniment" destroys all vermin instantaneously, without risk of injuring the animal, and the quadruped may be rinsed one minute after; no flea will remain alive: the skin will be thoroughly cleansed and the coat beautified. Dogs should never be allowed to suffer the torment imposed on them by these detestable vermin. If the owners could only realize the importance of ridding them of these ever noisome pests, there would be far less of snappishness, mange, fits &c. I have seen animals literally worried to death by fleas, perfectly exhausted, from incessant irritation, at last worn to a skeleton and gradually extinguished by a creeping consumption. Besides, who, (for his own personal comfort), would not rid his immediate vicinity of a worthless mob of blood-suckers awaiting the first favorable opportunity of regaling themselves on human blood. If your dog lie on straw, burn it once a week, as fleas harbor and propagate in the tubes of the straw. If the bed be carpet, or anything similar, let it be often cleansed or changed. Vermin revel in filth, and their extirpation depends mainly on cleanliness.

By attending to the general health of a dog, much disease may be avoided; indeed, this is far more essential than prescriptions for a cure. It is very easy to carry off a slight indisposition by gentle purgatives and a reformed diet; whilst confirmed disease is often difficult to combat, as few of the canine race can have the advantages which are ofttimes essential to their restoration. The eyes, the nose, the gums, the hair, the breath and particularly the character of the stools should be carefully noted. The eyes may be red or pale, sunken or protruded; the nose may be hot or dry or matted with dirt; the gums may be pale, &c. It will require bnt little experience to discover a disorganiza tion, which may be easily detected by him who has noticed the healthful appearance of the different parts and their variation under indisposition. When the bowels are swollen, it is generally an indication of worms, especially in puppies, who, if they are not attended to, may drop off, before they reach their fourth month. If you are in the habit of keeping your dog on the chain, let him at least run a few minutes every day. If he be kept in doors, he should also be allowed a little daily exercise outside. Change of air and diet will sometimes renovate, when all remedies fail; a change from city to country, from greasy meat to fresh milk, from a confined yard to the green fields, where he will generally recruit himself without the aid of medicine. Nature, (to whom Physicians are so deeply indebted for so many wonderful restorations), often effects a cure unaided, which might have defied the efforts of Apothecary's Hall. In summer, particularly, be careful to provide a supply of fresh water and a cool shelter from the sun. Never take your dog out, during the intense heat of the day; this is very apt to produce fits, often resulting in sudden death. Early in the morning is preferable for summer exercise. The kennel should be located in a shady spot during the summer; in winter it should be sheltered from the wind and so placed as to enable the dog to enjoy the sun shine, at will. Above all things, never chain a dog, where he cannot screen himself from the sun's rays. He must have the option of sunshine or shade; he should not be allowed to drink water, that has been standing in the sun or is otherwise damaged. If you should chance to forget to feed him for forty-eight hours, he would not run as much risk of injury, as during three hours of thirst, in hot weather. The best and cheapest dog-house may be made from a common packing-case; it will require nothing but a round hole, about six inches from the bottom, made just large enough to admit of the passage of the tenant; a frame with sufficient pitch should be made over the top, to be shingled or boarded for a roof, which should project all round, as much as convenient, to shelter the animal from the sun and rain. If the back or front part only, under the roof be enclosed, it will answer as a convenient depot for chain, collar, whip, comb, brush, mediçine, &c. There should be a piece of joice under

HARRIER.

HARRIER.

Favors the Foxhound and the English Beagle,
Just as the hawk resembles much the eagle;
The well known Harrier, pride of wealthy squires,
No hunter but his sportive stock admires.
Foxhound in color, but less high in limb,
Less elegant, less daring and less trim;
Of like endurance, not so swift of foot,
Of equal scent and cooler nerve to boot;
Well disciplined and mannerly, in fine,
No hunger tempts him on his game to dine;
But seized his prey, by long exciting run,
Restrains his appetite and feasts on fun.
Hie to the fields and scan the marshalled corps,
Of eager Harriers, forty, p'raps or more;
Onward they rush, when Pussey leads the way,
Away they stride, with mellow notes so gay;
While country bumpkins from the village crowd
The neighboring woods, and shout with voices loud;
Ascend the hill, the glad'ning hunt to view,
Again, again, their boisterous shouts renew.
Lo! here she comes, the fleet but jaded hare,
Struggling to gain some dark secluded lair,
Now closely pressed the hounds their prize must gain,
When Lepus springs in safety up a drain.

each end of the house, to keep it off the ground, in order to avoid dampness. In summer, an excavation, two or three feet in depth, should be made under it, and open at both ends, that the animal may have a cool retreat, during the heat. Those, who do not object to a trifling expense, may have the house posted on a large paving-stone, with an excavation under it, as before recommended. All burrowing animals seek the earth in hot weather; everything on the surface is heated; their instinct dictates to them the most reasonable method of sheltering themselves from the heat, at the same time. absorbing the cool exhalations from the ground. In southern climates, especially, this method is all important. In this manner, I have kept dogs from the polar regions, in comparative comfort, whilst many native-born and neglected have been scalded into fits, paralysis, rabies or hydrophobia. In the hot season, with young dogs, raw meats should be avoided, except it be quite fresh, and then it should not be over fed, especially to animals, who are debarred abundant exercise and excluded from their own natural medicine: grass. Nevertheless I have not perceived any evil effects from the mod-crate feeding of fresh sheep's heads, tripe or even entrails to animals of sufficient age and strength. A dog will thrive better on raw meat, than on any other food, and will grow larger: but he should be fed with discretion, and his health attended to, should his diet visibly disagree with him. He will grow fatter and be more healthy on moderate meals, than to be overgorged. The better plan is, to ascertain his average consumption and then allow him a little less. Keep his digestion in good order, and disease will rarely trouble him. His coat and ribs will generally indicate whether he be sufficiently cared for, whether he be sick or sound in his digestive organs. Feed him always in the same place, and at the same hour. Once a day is sufficient. if he be over six months old. By being fed only once a day, he is less choice, and will consume what he might refuse, if his appetite were dulled by a previous meal. Should you require him to be watchful at night, feed him in the morning; if you would have him quiet at night, feed him late, and don't leave him bones to gnaw. Dogs are pretty quiet, during the digestive process, when left to themselves, and should not have much exereise, after a heavy meal. They should only be lightly fed, before training-lessons, or on sporting-days; on the latter occasions, a little refreshment may be administered as occasion may require. Those kept in doors should be allowed to run a little after meals, when they generally require an evacuation. If a dog be regularly exercised, he will seldom even dirt around his kennel, and a healthy house-pet is rarely troublesome, except after eating. If a dog be dirty in the house, he should decidedly be broken of it, although he should not be corrected, unless he has had a fair opportunity of avoiding it. He should be invariably taken to the spot, be sufficiently twigged there, and unceremoniously scolded into the yard. It is important to catch him in the act, and administer summary chastisement. The punishment will be far more justly administered, if the animal be let out at regular intervals; this being done, he will not attempt to infringe the law, except in cases of dire necessity. Young puppies however, must be, in a measure excused or more gently corrected, as they are incapable of self-restraint. Nevertheless they may be very early initiated into habits of cleanliness. A

Dog is often spoiled, by being caressed by hundreds, and kicked by scores; either pampered by all, or fed by none; either constantly bound with a cramped range of a few feet, or left to ramble undirected, through the streets. He should have but one master; should not be rendered sullen and surly, for lack of associating with his superiors, neither should he be allowed an enlarged acquaintance, especially in his own neighborhood; as it will tend to render him listless as a guardian, and perchance too familiar with some, whose presence, it might be the peculiar interest of his master to avoid. Although there is as great a variety of talent and disposition in dogs, as in mankind, yet we can almost mould them, as we please. If they be too savage, they may be softened down by accustoming them to a variety of faces and friends; and correcting them in their fiery ebulitions. If too meek, their dispositions may be roused and their dormant passions excited; solitude, encouragement and occasional irritation may be resorted to; in fine, a tame listless temperament should be cautiously handled, yet continually fed with gentle irritants, and the animal will not long require *smarting up*. I thus have reduced the savage bull-dog to be as tractable as a hand organ, and have made the gentle Spaniel a thoroughly fierce watch-dog. We must use firmness, without severity, except in cases of conscious misdemeanor ; pass no dog-laws which we are not at all times prepared to enforce ; never punish for a fault, unless we are perfectly satisfied of guilt ; allow no one else to correct, unless urgent necessity demand it, and never allow the fire of our imagination to inflict more than deserved punishment.

Pups should be cautiously corrected, and although their obedience must of necessity be enforced, as early as they can distinguish between roast beef and stale bread, too much should not be exacted from them, and no severity used ; as it may have the effect of cowering them down, thus materially effecting their pluck and spirits in after life,

I am satisfied as a general rule, that a well amalgamated mixture of animal and vegetable, is the most healthful diet, for dogs of all ages, breeds and conditions. Dogs living in the house should on no account be fed on raw meat, as it gives them a very offensive smell and is in other respects very unsuitable.

TEETHING, TEETH &c.

A GREAT deal of stress is laid on the teething of dogs. About this period, Nature appears to be undergoing a certain change, and a dog is in less danger from dying from Distemper, after the operation is thoroughly effected. The animal of course becomes stronger, as he gets older; consequently the better fitted to withstand disease; otherwise the simple act of teething, I cannot imagine to effect materially the general health; although from the great excitability of delicate breeds of dogs, fits may be often attributed to the annoyance occasioned by the process of dentition. Until the teeth be fully developed, the animal will require more than ordinary care and attention. His stomach should never be overloaded, particularly with meat or any gross food. Of light fare however, he may always eat to the full, and his strength should be maintained by generous living. It is said there is great danger, should a puppy happen to swallow any of his teeth: For my part, I do not believe in any such nonsense, and should not be afraid to give a dog half a dozen with his dinner ; I am satisfied there would be no fatal result. It may be advisable to remove some of the first teeth, should any be in the way of the second crop, but I seldom see any occasion for it, except when they are quite loose, or interfere with the new-comers. Giving medicine to dogs simply because they are shedding their teeth is quite unnecessary. Should they be feverish or indisposed, it would be expedient, otherwise, Nature had better take its course. Dogs are apt to get cankered teeth, especially when attacked by Distemper, during the teething process ; therefore exposure to this latter disease should be avoided as much as possible, until the mouth is fairly furnished. The teeth often become foul and incrusted with Tarter. This arises either from gross feeding, the results of Distemper, or a disordered digestion, and is sometimes hereditary. Any good tooth-powder may be used and they may be cleaned with a brush. The ashes of burnt bread are about as good as anything for cleansing the teeth, and in no wise injurious. The teeth may be scraped, if necessary; but it should be done carefully, so as not to disturb the enamel. An occasional scrubbing with vinegar tends to sweeten the mouth and is excellent for cleansing the teeth. I do not imagine however, that cleansing the teeth will effectually cure fetid breath. It certainly has a good effect, but the stomach is more the seat of the affection, and must be kept healthy. Decayed teeth should be extracted as they render the breath very offensive. An animal with foul breath should be allowed but little meat, and be occasionally treated to a gentle purgative. Without attending to this, the teeth will soon become recoated, and the breath remain but little improved. For the age of a dog, we generally look to the teeth, but this is by no means a decided test, except perhaps at ages under two years. A five year old dog may perhaps have a better mouth than others of half his age. Nevertheless a young dog

BEAGLE.

BEAGLE.

With ears of Hound, and Turnspit limb to boot,
The gouty sportsman most inclined to suit;
Must some relation to the Turnspit be,
Else none with back, so long and low as he;
Black—tan, in color, tho' not ever so,
With Connoisseurs, the former all the go.
While yet the smallest of the hunting class,
But few his slow activity surpass;
His watchword "Onward," tardy tho' his pace;
His motto: "Slow and steady wins the race."
Rabbit or hare, in covert. apt to dodge,
From sheltered wall or thicket to dislodge,
And luckly after many a sinuous run,
Presents the victim to the fatal gun.
In slower times, in England widely known;
Of late, in Germany, more often grown.
When Hawk and Beagle graced the hunting
field,
'Ere yet the sun the pearly dew revealed,
In days of Wassail and of good old Sack,
Away they sped, the merry tuneful pack.
The lusty Baron, and the portly Squire,
Th' embroidered Lordling and the bloated Friar,
In concert joined, to greet the rising morn,
The gladdening echo of the inspiring horn.

may generally be distinguished from an old one by the lack of wear in the small front teeth. and from the clear whiteness of the teeth in general. The small front teeth are the first to give way; indeed some dogs (those of the short-nosed breeds especially) are apt to lose them at a very early age. If all were fed alike the teeth would more fairly indicate the years. but an animal, who has had to grind bones for a living, will file off more ivory in three days than the ordinary wear and tear of a decently fed animal, in a year. Long-nosed dogs generally have the best, the longest and most durable teeth, whilst the small front teeth of the snub-nosed are set so lightly in their sockets. that they are easily dislodged. This is more peculiar to Bull-dogs, King Charles' Spaniels and Pugs. Those fed on warm food and faring principally on rich meats will show early symptoms of decaying teeth. Close confinement. lack of exercise and a too nutritious diet tend to destroy the healthy tone of the system, consequently must be injurious to the teeth. Fetching stones is the most injurious of all things and should never be permitted, as it not only destroys the teeth, but the animal who is allowed the pastime is generally at the beck and call of every one, makes a perfect fool of himself, and will own any one for a master

CROPPING, TAILING, DEW-CLAWS.

THE dog-fancying portion of the community are so accustomed to the cropping of Bull-dogs, Terriers, Bull-terriers and others of the pugnacious class, that the public, through them, have become convinced that the operation is absolutely indispensible.

The practice originated in a desire to save the ears of the animal from being lacerated and torn, and to prevent them serving as a hold in his warlike encounters with others of the same stamp. It is decidedly an injurious practice, often producing hardness of hearing, if not deafness, by exposing the ear to the reception of all kinds of filth and tending to produce disease. I certainly am accustomed to think it improves the appearance of some breeds of dogs, but I believe they would be less punished, even in a fight, with their ears on; as the bite on a short ear would consequently be nearer the head, and on that account the more punishing. As for their being torn by thorns and otherwise damaged, the flaps are the greatest protection against all internal injuries. The method I adopt in cropping. is first to cut the top off one ear to the desired length; the piece taken off to be used as a measure, by which to cut the other top. When both tops are off. flatten the ear out with one hand and cut in a straight line from the base of the ear to the farthest point at the top, cutting of course both ears exactly alike. Do not cut too close in at the base, if you do not wish to subject the dog to great discomfort, for the sake of fashion. There are various methods of cropping, but whichever you adopt. be careful to cut both ears exactly alike, or the beauty of the handsomest animal may be ruined for life. It should be done with a large sharp scissors, so as to be effected with one cut; thus it will be better done and give the animal less pain. But never attempt the operation, unless you have a steady holder, as on this depends perhaps more than on your own skill. If the ears should be left long, or appear to be inclined to droop, they may be tied together for a few days, over the head by a piece of thread, passed through the ends of the ears with a needle. After the operation, strong salt and water will stay the bleeding and stop the smarting. A little olive oil may be afterwards put on twice a day, with a light feather ; but the ears will do about as well, if let alone. Some advocate the cutting of the ears, when the animal is only a few weeks old, True, they very soon heal under the mother's care, and the sooner on account of their tenderness, but I prefer waiting till the dog is four or five months old, because the ear is not developed at such an early age ; therefore in its growth, it becomes naturally thick, and seldom looks well ; in the second place, before the ears be cut, the natural droop has to be considered, and they should be shortened accordingly, or they will never stand up right. Besides in case of sickness or more especially Fits, it may be advantageous to have ears to cut off, to relieve the flow of blood to the head. As to tailing, it is a very simple operation (now almost out of fashion) and requires nothing but a knife or any sharp instrument, with which the *narrative* may be *abbreviated* to suite the taste of the owner. It is far preferable that this be done when young, as the tail is more difficult to heal than the ear. To stop the flow of blood, if necessary, put salt and vinegar in a rag and tie it over the end of the tail. There is no need of this, when the animal is very young; when more matured, however, I have seen several instances, where the animal would have bled to death without it. If you cut it when young, take care not to leave it too short, as it will not grow in proportion to other parts of the body, and a short stump is a most inelegant appendage to the most symmetrical form.

Dew-claws are considered by many as a proof of impurity of breed. I see no ground for such a supposition, as I have found them occasionally on all breeds, good, bad or indifferent, and I must say I cannot account for their appearance. They may, however, have once been the distinctive mark of a pure stock. Those who have any objection to them can easily remove them with a sharp scissors. They are generally very lightly attached, and the pain must be very trifling, especially when the animal is young.

CASTRATION OF DOGS.—SPAYING OF SLUTS.

CASTRATION is one of the most simple operations, requiring nothing more than a sharp knife, a steady hand and a little experience. The most suitable age, I consider to be from five to nine months. For this operation, the animal should be made perfectly secure, by one person holding his head, and a second the legs, whilst the hands of the operator must be perfectly free. If the dog's head be put into a bag, or be otherwise covered, he will be far less restive, or perhaps wholly unconscious of any danger. For all painful operations, a dog should be blinded ; it will detract greatly from his nervous restlessness and materially facilitate the process. The skin at the base of the testicle should be firmly held between the thumb and finger of the left hand, so as to present a fair tightened surface; then cut through the skin just deep enough to expose it to view. Whilst you still hold perfectly fast with the left hand, draw out the testicle, string and all with the right. Should it be difficult to draw out, the knife may be passed round it, to facilitate the extraction, but if the operation be performed at an early age, this will seldom be requisite, as the pressure of the thumb and finger will suffice to force the testicle out so as to present a fair hold for the right hand. Should the string not draw out, it may be cut off; of course each must be taken out separately; the same means used in extracting the first, applies also in the second. The operation should not be performed either during very warm or cold weather, unless the animal can be kept in a somewhat moderate degree of warmth, for at least a couple of weeks. No after-application is required, other than washing the parts, with strong salt and water, immediately after the operation, and a little lard or goose-grease, to soothe the irritation. The dog should be kept cool, quiet and cheerful; his food should not be gross, and he may require a little cooling physic. He should be exposed to no extremes

ENGLISH GREYHOUND.

ENGLISH GREYHOUND.

His sinewy limb, symmetric form and grace,
Vie with the hind, and equal him in pace ;
Elastic, bounding o'er the flowery mead,
Unmatched his spring, agility and speed.
His color black or white, red, blue or grey ;
The latter, the original, they say ;
Long tapering nose, small ear and piercing eye,
His destined game unerringly descry.
With common hound, disdains to scent his prey ;
By sight alone, he speeds his light'ning way ;
The trembling hare, for safety flies in vain,
And fruitless seeks the shelt'ring copse to gain.
On Albion's shore, where hunting is the rage,
His feats and pedigree grace every page ;
Grandsire and Grandam, all is there recorded,
And to the fleetest, is the prize awarded.
If ought impure, in blood or limb, we trace,
His name's ignored, excluded from the race ;
Condemned a Lurcher, fit for Poacher's game,
But for the nobler sports, despised his name.
And many a hero, famed for martial deeds,
Vaunts his fleet greyhounds, and his rampant
steeds ;
And when in glee, the sparkling wine they sup,
Points to Diana's prize, the "Golden Cup."

of either heat or cold, be allowed very little exercise and be kept in a perfectly clean place, that no dirt may enter the sore. The changes produced by this operation differ in different subjects; as a general thing, its results are fat and a lazy independence, and of course in all cases a perfect indifference to the charms of the other sex. I am inclined to believe that if these *altered* subjects were not allowed to get too fat, they probably would retain more of their natural vigor. I am far from believing that it detracts either from their sagacity or intelligence. I have seen several cases, where it has added to their pluck and daring. These may be quoted as exceptions. They are decidedly less inclined to roving, are more cleanly in their habits and the more easily recovered, if lost.

The Spaying of Sluts is not much practiced now-a-days. The effect on them is about the same as on the male. I have witnessed the operation, but have never performed it. It consists in making an incision in the flank, and extracting the ovaries, which renders the animal incapable of producing young. It requires a practiced hand to ensure success; I shall therefore not enlarge on the subject.

DOG-TRAINING, TRICKS, &c.

INTRODUCTORY REMARKS ON THE TRAINING OF DOGS.

One might suppose from the surprise and astonishment expressed, on the relation of examples of the extraordinary sagacity, instinct and reasoning powers of the dog, that these gifts were bestowed by Nature only on the favored few; whilst the majority of canines were far beneath the level of ordinary brutes and actually incapable of instruction, denied the privilege of ranking among their more favored brethren. This impression however is not altogether groundless, considering how few persons there are, who take into consideration the evils, to which they are personally subjected, through the lawless multitude of untutored quadrupeds, with which the whole country is infested, or who pause to imagine the benefits which might revert to themselves, did they contribute their share, towards ameliorating the condition of animals, who are ever willing to serve and doubly blest in obeying.

Mr. Smith envies Mr. Jones, because Mr. J. is the owner of such a well-behaved, intelligent, respectable dog, and wonders where he got the breed. Mr. White can't imagine how his neighbor Green could have taught his dog so many curious tricks, and is anxious to get a puppy of the same stock, which of course he expects will educate himself, at a very early age.

My object is to prove that it requires but a small amount either of time or labor, to rescue even the meanest mongrel from a life of degradation and misery and place him in a position, where he may be respected for his virtues and appreciated for his worth.

The most important points to be considered in the training of a dog are first: to understand somewhat of his natural disposition and temperament. Secondly: not to exact too much of him at once. Thirdly: to use as little force as possible. Fourthly: always to insist on obedience and never to pass unnoticed the slighest act of insubordination. Fifthly: begin your instructions as early as possible.

(The pup is never too young to learn, especially to do wrong, if left to himself.)

The principal causes of so many dogs being spoiled in the training may be traced to their having been taken in hand too late; having had too many masters, from the indecision or severity of their instructors. The moment a dog is known to fetch, three or four objects are thrown at once, and every acquaintance amuses himself in putting the abilities of the animal to the test; he is consequently puzzled, considers it only a play-game and becomes remiss in his duty to his master. Just so with any of his other performances. He is perhaps allowed to follow a variety of persons, which often tends to lessen his attachment and obedience to his real owner, at the same time allowing him favorable opportunities of committing a variety of acts, which he dared not dream of, in his master's presence. A dog then to be rightly trained, should be under the sole management of one person; he should be allowed to do nothing without his master's knowledge and consent. He should be expressly habituated to all kinds of company, hogs, cows, dogs, goats, sheep, chickens, &c., so that he may be firmly checked by his master, should he attempt any wanton attacks on others of the animal kingdom, at the same time that he may be taught to rid himself of all fear of their presence by occasionally associating with them. The earliest impulse of a canine, that has any pretension to pluck, is to attack the first animal he sees, whilst all dogs, either with or without evil intent are inclined to pursue every living creature that runs from them. This inclination can either be encouraged or checked, either speedily annihilated or cultivated, to suit the will of the trainer ; therefore it necessarily follows. that as soon as a dog has a will of his own, it should be well directed or immediately curbed. If he be old enough to eat, he is old enough to be made to let it alone ; if he be old enough to come when called and go away when he is bid, he is also old enough to know his place, and be made to stay there, till he is wanted, (at least in his master's presence.) But in these early lessons, we must be extremely careful to keep in perfect good humor, and to let our punishments be very light ; as there is not only great danger in forcing too much on weak intellects, but in inflicting too much on youthful pets. Let your lessons be light, easy, short and pleasant. If your pupil tires, adjourn the meeting. By consulting his feelings, he will be more apt and willing, will delight in your teachings and long for their repetition.

Half a pound of encouragement, two ounces of decided disapproval, a quarter of a pound ot patience and two ounces of gentle correction, form an excellent mixture as a basis for canine instruction. I have trained many dogs for my own private use, and I confess they have caused me anything but trouble; they have been all extremely apt, docile and willing. I do not attribute this to their superior intellectual proportions, neither to any inborn sagacity of my own, but merely to a method of consulting their inclinations and exciting their wills, thus rendering their toil a pleasure, their studies a sport. The teachings, (as I often observe) should be short, often, and regular. A quarter of an hour twice a day will be of more effect than two hours three times a week. The best place, (for early lessons especially) is in a yard or moderate sized enclosure, as the animal will be far more obedient, where he has no chance of escape, and his attention will not be diverted by other objects. He had better also be taught alone, until he is well advanced, as I have observed dogs to be very shy at first in performing in the presence of others. The Trainer should also appear very joyous when the student does his duty. This has a most astonishing effect; as dogs (being no hypocrites themselves,) judge entirely from appearances, and look one right in the face, which to them is the unerring index of the mind. When you unchain a dog to give him a lesson, always let him have a good romp first, (if he please), as he will generally be uneasy, if you omit it, consequently less attentive to your instructions. If possible, never allow any one to help you teach him; he will readily digest the commands of one, whilst a second method is apt to puzzle him; besides he will always be more tractable under one instructor, and will far more readily obey the teachings of his master. Any strange system of management will only tend to diminish his attachment and obedience. By these remarks, I do not mean to infer that a man is bound to train his own dog, neither that an animal might not be better educated by two persons, than by one only, who in a measure either neglected him, or treated him improperly; but, that the animal is the more easily managed, when directed by one head, and owned solely by one master. With regard to Sporting Dogs, I consider it advisable that they should be trained rather by regular Sporting men, than to be spoiled by a youthful *Greenhorn*. A regular Breaker is better enabled to give him constant practice in the field of his future labors, than the occasional Sportsman, in whose keeping he may become addicted to bad habits. Another thing, he should, if convenient, be raised in the country, where he will become more healthful, vigorous and hardy; that is to say, unless the owner should have other means at hand of securing to him that sanitory exercise, indispensably necessary to his perfect physical and mental development. Dogs in some respects are like children. Show me a dozen genteel children raised in the city, pampered with delicacies, exercising themselves in the nursery, carefully cloaked and india-rubbered, on the slightest fall of the barometer, thus fattening the Doctor and Apothecary at the expense of their delicate constitutions. Compare with them a dozen Rustics. Who will throw a stone the farthest, climb a tree the

ITALIAN GREYHOUND.

ITALIAN GREYHOUND.

Model of beauty, symmetry and grace,
From fair Italia springs thy sylphlike race;
Sweet emblem of the clime, that gave thee birth,
Symbol of action, sprightliness and mirth!
Like his famed compeer of the nobler grade,
Of different color, and of varied shade;
Matchless in mould, of fawnlike form and limb;
Small silken ear. soft, light, transpar nt skin,
Fitted alone in genial warmth to dwell—
Genteel appendage of the flaunting Belle.
His magic trip and quick, elastic bound,
Disgrace the awkward step of meaner hound;
The gay attendant of the proud and fair,
To doubt his use or merit none shall dare.
The maiden's nursling and the bride's delight,
Fondled by day, and feathered up at night;
For ruder sports, inapt his slender form,
Yet quick of ear, the stealthy rogue to warn,
In courage lacking, yet his very fear
Will rouse the house when thief or burglar's
near.
Then wonder not, a pampered hound like he,
So delicate, effeminate should be;
His graces charm, nor let his faults perplex,
Since he was framed to please the gentler sex.

quickest, or stand toil the best? Just so with animal nature in other forms. Again, I repeat, wholesome food, plenty of air and exercise are the principal ingredients necessary to frame a hardy and enduring constitution, and the safest antidotes against degeneration and disease.

DOWN! STOP! STEADY THERE!

DOWN! Gently press the dog down, repeating "*Down! Down Sir!*" hold over him a twig or a whip; if he resist. (as most probably he may,) use the whip very lightly, and increase in severity, according to the obstinacy of the animal, whilst you carefully exhibit firmness without anger. As soon as he has remained "*Down*" about half a minute, do not omit to encourage and play with him, give him a little rest, and repeat. As soon as you see he understands it, make him perform without the sign of the whip, raising only the hand over him. (The whip may be concealed in your pocket. and produced in case of necessity.) When he *lowns* without threatening, try him at a little distance from you, (say six feet). If he refuse at that distance, approach him, administering a little correction, and repeat, till a polite request be sufficient to enforce compliance. Be cautious not to weary him, by repeating the same thing too often. Change off to a *fetching*, or any other lesson. Keep up his spirits by constant encouragement, and appear to join in the fun, though always maintaining your authority. When he *downs* short at six feet, or at any distance from you, change your command "Down" to "*Stop! Down!*" The hand uplifted the same, and go on increasing the distance, little by little, always enforcing the "*Stop*" till it becomes instantaneous. Continue this, till he is perfect at a distance, equal to the full extent of your voice. When he is in motion, omit now the word "*Down*," and only use "*Stop*." This being effected, accustom him to stop, when he is on the full run; throw an object for him to fetch, and occasionally stop him short, when at the height of his speed. Then set him at some animal, and before he quite reaches him, check him short with the "*Stop*." Don't weary him by a too oft repetition of the same thing. The next thing is to make him stay, under the word "*Stop*" till he is permitted to move; and he never should at any time be allowed to stir, unless invited by the signal "Up." At first, of course, a very short time must be exacted, (say half a minute) at the expiration of which he must be released by the signal "Up" accompanied by raising the hand, invitingly called away and encouraged; but be the time ever so short, he must never be allowed to leave of his own accord. By gradually increasing his time, and unerringly enforcing your orders, you may eventually succeed in keeping him there for hours, if you wish. I have occasionally forgotten my own orders, and have found my faithful dog, true to his post, hours after the command of "*Steady there*" was issued. This is the word now to be used. Remember then "*Down,*" "*Stop,*" "*Up*" *and* "*Steady there.*"

COME IN! KEEP IN! GO ON!

UNLESS a dog come, when he is called, he is not to be depended on. He may be tempted either for sport, malice, or pastime to pursue a cat, hog, dog, &c.; worse than that, he may be inclined to dodge after the opposite sex, regardless of his master's commands, deaf to his threats and entreaties. As a barrier against such casualties, he should be strictly taught to come immediately at call. Now this cannot be classed among dog-tricks, but perhaps it is more difficult to teach, as it requires considerable judgment to enforce, and often great patience to forbear. A dog must be taught to come, with as little threatening as possible, especially when he is at a distance, as young dogs may easily be too much intimidated by threats. When a command has to be obeyed at a distance, its execution depends principally on the animal's will. He should then be humored, until he thoroughly understands his duty, after which he will bear such seasonable correction, as the case may require. He should be regularly drilled into it, at gradually increasing distances. A beckoning sign should also be made accompanying the command, or a peculiar whistle used, more particularly if he be a sporting dog, who may be often out of sight. It is convenient that he should understand both sign, voice and whistle. His obedience should be

POINTER.

POINTER.

In color, size, to Setter most akin ;
With him contends Diana's prize to win ;
Of form more elegant, when highly bred,
Smooth drooping ear and intellectual head ;
Of nervous build and muscular in limb,
Clear, close set coat, with tail, long, straight
and slim ;
In England, Scotland, Ireland, France and Spain,
Varying in feature, yet in worth the same ;
By some, the Setter is the worthiest deemed ;
By others, Pointers are the most esteemed ;
But, 'ere deciding, we should first compare
Climate and treatment, management and fare.
The former thickly clad, by Nature warm,
Adapted best, to brave the cold and storm.
Through bush and bramble, fearless cleaves his
way,
Deep rushing waters must his steps obey ;
The Pointer flags not, in the burning heat,
Nor jaded, pants, the cooling spring to greet ;
Solely, wholly, purely, all for fun,
His aim is centered, in the double gun.
Unlike the Hound, he hunts not to destroy ;
The sportsman's glory is his highest joy ;
In fine, in gaming powers, so like the Setter,
A task it were, to nominate the better.

thoroughly tested in every way, and his habits of *willing submission* indelibly confirmed.

"*Keep in*" is also essential to the good manners and safety of your dog. It keeps him from wandering off at undesirable periods, and enables him to wind his way through a crowd, without losing his master. He should not be allowed to go on, without the order "*On, Go on.*" If he should show a determination to advance, he may be saluted with a gentle tap, to the tune of "*In, Keep in!*" At first, he should not be kept in too long at a time, but often encouraged by the word "*On.*" If he refuse to go on, he may be excited by throwing a cracker &c., a little ahead.

Remember, although he may be forced to come *in*, it is extremely difficult to *force* him to *go on*, until he is thoroughly drilled. This must therefore be effected principally by encouragement and good humor, sometimes by patting and exciting, or even by advancing at a quick pace yourself. In all these things, the disposition of the animal must regulate in a great measure our method of treatment. One thing is certain, the more he is pleased with you, the more readily will he obey.

SHAKING HANDS; RIGHT HAND; LEFT HAND; SITTING UP; STANDING UP; WALKING ON THE HIND LEGS.

GENERALLY, the dog's first act of friendship is to put up his *hand* to his master. His paw should be taken and gently shaken; then the other; at the same time, repeating "*right hand*" for the right, and "*left hand*" for the left, always taking the one required, and invariably refusing the other. Your hand should be first extended to the side of the paw demanded, so that the other paw cannot reach it. He will soon become habituated to the words right and left, and immediately distinguish between them. He may then be taught (if you please) to go round and shake hands with the .whole company. To make it perhaps more amusing, you may term the right paw the gentlemen's and the left the lady's; or you may while standing up, hold out both your hands, inviting him to jump up. When he has done this a few times, you can, while your hands are out, say "Show me how you shake hands with the ladies" when the act of giving both paws, will be the answer.

To make a dog sit up, he must be placed in position, and be there made to sit for a short time and seriously threatened, should he dare to disobey the order "*Sit up Sir.*" He must be kept a very short time at first and his poorest efforts must be flattered. Although at the outset, he must be placed in position, he should soon be taught to rise at a touch, accompanied by the word of command, and shortly after by the word alone. A gentle rap on his fore-feet with a twig may be of occasional service. When he answers to the word, you should increase your distance from him, be more peremptory in your orders, and rather more severe, if he disobey. He may then, at a short distance have a pipe placed in his mouth and a cap on his head; he may also be ornamented with a pair of spectacles, which together with a newspaper, placed before him, will render him well worthy of your attention.

As for teaching an animal to stand up on his hind legs, a piece of meat will be found quite sufficient inducement. This is the most natural and simple method of instruction. As he stands up to reach the meat, it should be drawn slowly forward, for him to follow on his hind legs, while at the same time, you repeat "*Walk along Sir.*" You may find it easier perhaps, to start him from a wall, against which he must be stood upright, and tempted onward in hopes of the meat, of which he should be allowed a small portion, when he behaves well, but *never* unless to reward him for his efforts of obedience. Of course he will require no regular fee, when he thoroughly understands his duty, although an occasional kindness will at no time be thrown away.

FETCHING, CARRYING, SEEKING, FINDING.

Nearly all dogs, (especially in their puppish days) have a natural propensity of running after objects and carrying them about. I have rarely met with an exception ; it appears to be the instinctive pastime of the whole canine fraternity. There can be no difficulty therefore, in cultivating an instinct so amusing ; no barrier to directing it to pleasing and useful results. The first lesson must be perfect play. A ball, a piece of wood, or anything easy to grasp and not injurious to the teeth, should be thrown a little way. As soon as the pupil has picked it up, he must be tempted, (if possible), to carry it back to his master. Should he not return to him with it, it should be gently taken out of his mouth, and again thrown, exciting the dog a little between the acts. It should invariably be *taken* out of his mouth. If he persist in holding it fast, tap his nose, saying, "*Let go Sir*," to make him relax his hold; at the same time keep hold of the object, till he gives way. Then praise him and play with him a little. As he progresses, send the object farther and insist on his restoring it to you. Remember this: in training a dog, no more punishment must be administered, than *just enough* to answer the purpose. Recollect also, that the less of reprimand you can get along with, the better. I have observed a general defect in all trained dogs; they are too "*hard broken*;" have been taught more to fear than to respect. See how sneakingly they crouch at their master's threat! This should not be. They should be engaged, as far as possible, to yield a willing obedience. A dog will show his style of education, as perceptibly as a child, and the method pursued in his training is calculated either to secure to him a career of comfort and enjoyment, or to impregnate his every movement, with a sneaking timidity, degrading to the brute and disreputable to his master. When he fetches well and is carrying the object in his mouth, walk off, calling him to follow you. Do not go too far, before you take it from him; then give it to him again and go a little farther. Should he drop it, make him pick it up again, which if he refuse, replace it in his mouth, and make him carry it again, and still go on, *never omitting* either to make him pick it up, or to replace it in his mouth yourself, every time he may drop it. Avoid his dropping it at all, if you can, by not allowing him to carry it too far at first. When you are satisfied that he knows his duty, he may be corrected a little or scolded upon every transgression. A basket may now be given him to carry, the handle of which must be placed straight in his mouth. He must then follow with it. It should be taken from him at short intervals at first, (every time praising him up), gradually increasing the distance as before, and occasionally, should he drop it, he may be made to feel his transgression. At all events, whenever he drops it, he must be impressed with a consciousness of wrong. The severity of the punishment must be graded according to the merciful judgment of the owner. Often a severe lecture will give great effect to a light chastisement. The basket should be thrown for him to fetch, and should he take hold of it wrong, the handle should be presented to him, that he may take it off the ground.

Seeking and Finding, are also very easy to teach a dog, already initiated in fetching and carrying. In order to effect this, when you have thrown anything, hold your pupil, a little, before you let him fetch it ; first of all a very short time and at a very short distance, increasing little by little both time and space. This being fairly accomplished, throw the object where he cannot see it, repeating the same means. Should he not find it immediately, pretend to help him look after it, even pointing it out to him, if necessary. Make him follow you with it a little ; then take it out of his mouth, drop it, unknown to him, and excite nim by "Look about" till he find it. Continue this exercise of dropping, until he is perfectly familiarized to it. After this, drop or place the object in any spot, holding him in view of it at the same time; then take him off a short distance, but out of sight; whisper to him "*Fetch it*" and let him go, that he may bring it to you. You may reduce all your commands to a whisper, if the whisper be used conjointly with the regular word of command. In this manner, he is made clearly to understand, from having had a previous indication of your will. By dropping an article and causing him to fetch it, at graduated distances, he may be trained to retrieve at any length. In order to render this more effectual, introduce him occasionally to your pocket-book, gloves, handkerchief, cane, &c. Of course he will the more readily recognize these objects than other strange articles, and when dropped, he will never fail to recover them.

GOING INTO AND FETCHING OUT OF THE WATER. DIVING.

SOME dogs have such a desire for aquatic adventures, that they require only the sight or

SETTER.

SETTER.

Red, brown, or orange, liver, white or black;
P'raps black or tan, or mottled on the back;
Little it matters, what his hue, or shade,
If finely cast, and well proportioned made.
Such strange varieties spring up of late,
Perchance 't were vain, his salient points to
state;
Ear drooping low, with neatly feathered hair;
Light flowing tail, and legs well fringed with
care;
Bright serious eye, black nose, nor sharp, nor
round,
Unlike Italian or King Charley hound;
Something in shape, in pattern and in mould,
Like a Newfoundland, about six months old.
Tho' none but sportsmen dare his merits scan,
'Tis he, the choicest pastime gives to man;
He finds the Plover, Woodcock, Snipe and Rail;
He points the Grouse, the Pheasant, Partridge,
Quail;
Like a trained Rifleman, he threads his way,
But sudden halts, to mark his destined prey;
With foot, well poised, and every nerve astrain,
He holds his breath and stills his every vein;
With powerful nerve, his struggling will denies,
Firm as a rock th' enchanted victim eyes;
The fluttering game alone his bonds release,
Or echo of the fatal fowling piece.

perhaps smell of the water, in moderate weather, to invite them in. The Newfoundland and Spaniel appear to have the strongest instinctive desire for swimming, though even some of these require considerable encouragement and training, to make them good water-dogs. I have however never raised a dog msyelf, whether Newfoundland, St. Bernard, Spaniel, Terrier, &c., without having easily imparted to him a particular fondness for the water. Greyhounds, thin-coated and hairless dogs are the most backward, on account of their light covering and chilly nature. I have known hardy Bull-terriers to face the ice, better than a Newfoundland, no doubt to be accounted for by their dauntless courage and determination, rather than by their fitness to resist the cold. A large dog is the more easily taught it, when young, than a pup of smaller breed, as he can venture farther, without getting out of his depth. The first lesson should be in shallow water, or if deep, of very gentle descent, as young dogs are often checked, on finding themselves too suddenly out of their depth. The pupil must be very gradually introduced to the watery element, by casting the object to be fetched, into shallow water, close to the bank, and taking it immediately out of his mouth on landing. The distance must be daily increased, according to the aptness of the scholar. Care should be taken to make the lessons very short, until he is far enough advanced in practice, to venture freely of his own accord ; even then it is injurious to prolong too much the exercise, on account of disgusting the animal, or causing him to be too much chilled or exhausted. A dog should upon no consideration be thrown into the water, unless you are positively satisfied he can never be tempted to venture alone. It will serve at any rate to purify his pelt, but will never make him a water-dog. Hundreds, who might have made good water-dogs, are ruined, by being forced against their will, and thereby scared at the very idea of drinking out of a pond. When you begin your instructions, let it be in warm summer weather, that the dog may feel a real pleasure in cooling himself off. If you commence in cold weather, you may set your dog against it, by his disagreeable early impressions ; therefore begin in shallow-water, and in warm weather, and let his introductory initiations be short, easy and very encouraging.

He must be taught to dive on the same graduated principle. Let the object thrown, be a first barely under water, increasing its depth, according to progress. By way of practice, a tub may be used, and a piece of meat thrown into it, that he may be taught to immerse the whole head. In learning to fetch from the bottom of the water, the same article should be thrown, which he is perfectly willing to fetch on land, that he may be the more eager to take it. In spite of all our endeavors, entreaties, remonstrances and threats, some animals appear to be almost bomb proof, against diving lessons; when such is the case, their talents should be diverted in another channel. Anything that sinks gradually in the water is the best to teach with, as on seeing it sink, the animal will be the more likely to dip after it. A basket slightly weighted will answer this purpose. A duck will be found occasionally serviceable. One of his wings should be clipped a little, that he may be compelled to dive, in order to escape. But even a duck will not always dive. Whilst a dog is swimming, only one object should be allowed to engage his attention at once, which he should invariably be induced to bring ashore. If he miss it, a stone should be thrown to point out the spot. But to assist in these swimming lessons, there is nothing like a well-trained water-dog; he will teach your beginner more swimming in ten minutes, than you can urge on him in a week. Dogs who indicate no aqueous desire whatever, will often suddenly change their ideas, when another leads the way, especially if the latter be a companion. When once thoroughly initiated, he is far better alone, as in fetching together, they are apt to get in each other's way, and are likewise rather subject to quarrel. A live rat to a rat dog or others is a great temptation. Any other animal demonstration may be devised, should the canine prove unwilling from ordinary excitants.

GOING UP STAIRS, GOING DOWN STAIRS, KEEPING OUT OF DOORS, STAYING IN DOORS.

THESE are very simple things to teach, and as easily understood by the most ordinary of canine intellects. Here, the teacher's coaxing.

is of little service. At first a person should be posted at the top of the stairs, whilst the master stands at the bottom with his dog. The former must call whilst the latter seconds him by saying " *Go up stairs Sir*," and if necessary should add the twig to his gentle rebukes, in which case the student will be delighted to escape the blows, to rush to the protection of a friend. This repeated a few times, acompanied with the command " *Up stairs*," &c., will soon be thoroughly understood, after which the word alone will be sufficient, and by practice even a whisper. If he be slow of comprehension or backward in obedience, your friend at the top of the Stairs may tempt him with a light refreshment. The "*Down stairs Sir*," may be effected in the same way, simply by reversing the position of master and assistant. Recollect, practice makes perfect, and that good humor will ensure constant obedience, while severity and crabbedness are forbidding to the whole animal creation. Accustom your dog to signs, accompanying his every act of submission, and test him often by a whisper. Your distance from the stairs may be increased, according to progress. To keep a dog from entering a house, when the door is open. keep in some suitable spot, a long twig or whip ; let it suddenly remind him, that he is decidedly out of place. Say nothing to him, till after the stripe is given, and then simply "*Out.*" If the family agree to this method of treatment, a few simple cracks will not fail to keep him in his place ; but, if invited in, he will not fail to take advantage of the indulgence, in the absence of his monitors. The door should be occasionally left open, in order to test him, whilst a person is concealed close by, ready to administer chastisement unawares. This will be effectual, as he will always be suspicious, when no one is at hand. He should also be tempted by a visitor, to walk in for a piece of meat, when he should be suddenly checked by an unseen hand, so that eventually no temptation will be of any avail, and the choicest viands will be secure from his attacks. In the city especially, it will be well to keep your dog from going out, when the street-door is open. This may be effected by using the same means, in the street, that are recommended for the house. A stranger should tempt him outside, whilst the master is in ambush to greet him with a twig and the word "*In.*" The door may now and then be left open, whilst the dog is watched and effectually taught that he must not go out, without his master, or a privileged inmate of the house.

JUMPING THROUGH A HOOP; OVER A STICK, &C. DOWN DEAD. STAND FIRE.

"NECESSITY is the mother of invention," particularly so, where the digestive organs are at stake. The safest and most expeditious method of teaching a dog how to jump through a hoop, is to hold a piece of meat, on the other side of it, denying him all other access to it, except by going through. The hoop must be so held or placed, that he can neither get over, under or round. At first he may be awkward, and blunder through it, but necessity and practice will soon make him expert. As he progresses, the temptation may be withdrawn; still a stranger should not be allowed to practice him, without paying his fee.

When the dog has been taught to lie down at command, he must be made to remain stretched at full length and severely threatened, if he offer to stir. He must then be pulled along by the tail and then by the leg, whilst you still insist on his perfect and motionless submission, which must absolutely be enforced at all hazards. This must be repeated in short and easy doses, until he remains perfectly still. Although this lesson will require great firmness and decision, his temperature must be taken into serious consideration, for, if you do not keep him in decent humor, you will render him the more intractable. If therefore he be of the snappish caste, you should grade your exactions accordingly. You may also test his *deadness* by making him stand fire, while you strike all round him with a stick, call him by name, &c., but he must only rise at the word "*Up*." You may then use any expression you think proper terminating with the word "*Up*," when of course he will briskly start up, regardless certainly of the words preceding it. For instance: you may say "If thieves were in the house, I don't believe that dog would get "up." He will appear to understand it all, and spring up immediately. The word "*Up*" should be pronounced with emphasis enough to attract

WATER SPANIEL.

WATER SPANIEL.

Of him, the trifold merits we demand,
Of Pointer, Beagle and of Newfoundland ;
Active, intelligent, determined, spry,
In hunting qualities, with Hound may vie,
With Pointer, trace the Woodcock, Snipe or
Hare,
Or with Newfoundland, surging waters dare.
In form compact, in temper faultless too,
In pluck and vigilance excelled by few ;
Best of retrievers, in all climates good,
For river, swamp, or brake, or thorny wood,
Of liver color, oft'times mixed with white,
The king of Spaniels, if but tutored right ;
Largest of all, in limb more firmly set,
Fondest of all the Genus Canis yet ;
Robust in frame, with soft and curling hair,
Except the head, which should be somewhat
bare ;
An eye full beaming with expression kind,
Bespeaks his friendship and his truth combined;
An ear, with graceful ringlets drooping low,
His limbs well clad and feathered to the toe.
Although Dogographers oft' disagree,
Methinks his race original must be ;
Old England boasts the honor of his birth,
His fame acknowledged and esteemed his
worth.

his attention, and still not to make it appear intentional. He must be practiced with "Up and Down" till he obeys instantly. All sorts of exciting words may be addressed to him, when dead, but the teacher must on no account allow him to stir, except to one command. An assistant will be useful to excite him in every way to rise, while his master insists on perfect "*Dead.*" Be easy, firm and decided in your commands, and appear to be highly delighted in their execution, always allowing intervals for a frolic, between yourself and your pupil. You should never lose sight of this in your teachings. It is not so essential after the dog is thoroughly trained, but even then, it should be often resorted to, as an incentive to willing submission.

STEADY! WITH MEAT ON THE DOG'S NOSE. MEAT IN HIS MOUTH, NOT TO BE EATEN.

PLACE a piece of meat on the dog's nose; keep him steady with it there, till you have slowly counted "*ten,*" repeating fuller the last number "*Ten,*" after which, give him liberty to eat it. Repeat this manner, a few times; then make him keep perfectly still at the word "*Steady,*" without touching him, after which the counting alone will soon be sufficient. If he let it fall, before the *ten* is fully counted, he must be reprimanded or corrected and the operation resumed. During the lesson, he should have nothing given him, except after the word "*Ten.*"

This being got through with, you may allow him to take a bit of meat or anything nice in his mouth. At first, press his jaws gently, while you are counting; should he attempt to bite it, he must be checked and the pressure increased, repeating the word "*Steady.*" When the *ten* is up, allow him to swallow it. Repeat this, after the same fashion, till you are satisfied he knows his duty; after you may give him the bait in his mouth, trusting to his education alone. Again repeat, "*Steady*" and go on counting. Should he unfortunately swallow it, you must correct him according to your judgment, and commence another trial. As he becomes accustomed to his duty, you may count slower, and occasionally pause, to test his patience. To try him more severely, exercise him when you know he is hungry. In any of your teachings, should you find it necessary, you may keep the dog within bounds, by a chain and collar, although it should be avoided, as far as possible. Nevertheless, it may occasionally be indispensable, to restrain the unruly or to embolden the timid. With animals, whose early tuition has been neglected, it may be the more necessary, as a more decisive treatment is requisite, and in many cases, we need the absolute power of correction, without admitting a chance of retaliation or escape.

FETCHING FROM THE STORE. CARRYING TO A GIVEN POINT.

A DOG, well versed in ordinary fetching and carrying, will require only a little directing and discretionary management, to enable him to execute many little useful errands to a neighboring store, or even at a considerable distance. It would not be advisable to practice it much n the City, unless the animal is watched, as the poor creature runs a great risk of abuse, with out any chance of redress, and such an exposure might prove injurious both to his physical and mental developments, by deterring him from similiar adventures for the future, to say nothing of the risk of his coming in contact with a new master. The same means recommended for "*Going up and down stairs*" must be resorted to here. When he is taught to fetch the basket, it may be left in a Store or elsewhere, whence he should be made to fetch it out; (See "*Fetching*") first only at a short distance, and in sight. When this is done, a person in the store, should call the dog, who holds the basket in his mouth, while standing by his master, who orders him to go to the store, the person in the store should take the basket out of his mouth, and replace it shortly after, adding the word "Back" and giving him signs to return to his master, who should call him at the same time. After a few repetitions of *Backwards* and *Forwards*, aided by the second person, the owner may begin by sending him alone, not forgetting to finish with the word "*Store*," at every command. He should

COCKER SPANIEL.

COCKER SPANIEL.

In size fifteen, to thirty pounds betwixt;
Of liver color, or with white commixed;
Lively and gay, intelligent and spry;
Ears pendant, flowing hair, endearing eye:
For Snipe or Woodcock, Rail, and such like
game,
Well known his worth, indelible his fame;
Where Pointer, Setter cease their game to trace,
He rushes to their covert hiding place.
Like the Scotch terrier, threads his sinuous way,
Nor tangled briars, his onward movement stay;
Ever afield and ever in again,
Careful he scours the wood and scans the plain.
Returning oft', to seek his master's will;
Anxious his joyous mission to fulfil.
Look where you may, among the canine mass,
In scenting powers, the Cocker none surpass;
In learning apt, and fawning in his ways;
True in affection, sensitive to praise;
Excels in memory, passing fond of fire,
While yet for water, native, his desire.
If e'er to man, decreed a friend above,
His looks are fondness, and his actions love;
No treatment harsh, or cruel, or unjust,
Can e'er seduce him from his wonted trust.

invariably be encouraged by both parties and occasionally have a penny to spend for himself. When he goes entirely on his own account, another and a different kind of basket should be used, so that he may be taught to distinguish between his own private affairs and the business of his master. A penny may be wrapped up, which he may be sent to lay out for himself, which of course, should be spent for something eatable. If he were taught this invariably at regular hours, he would as certainly come at the appointed time for his penny, as for his regular meals. By this simple way of training, a dog may be rendered highly serviceable, in the country; he can fetch the milk from a neighboring farm, supply the kitchen with wood, do all the little errands at the store, and make himself generally useful. Much time need not be devoted to educate an animal thoroughly; constant habit and experience will work wonders on him. Only feed a dog three days in succession, at the same hour, if you omit the fourth, you may be sure he will remind you of it. Correct him three times for the same transgression, and he will scarcely ever require another reprimand. His memory surpasses in many things, that of the human race, and he is alike the creature of habit and circumstance. Let your lessons be short and regular ; make them as pleasing and exciting as you can, and your pupil will always be up and ready, cheerful and willing to execute either your nod or your whisper. Is it not worth while to rise a quarter of an hour earlier (if necessary) for a few months, to educate a faithful friend, who will be rendered the happier, by devoting his whole life to your useful service.

TEACH YOUR DOG TO CALL YOU, AT A REGULAR HOUR.

ALTHOUGH the Dog may be considered disinterested in his affection and fidelity to his owner, he is nevertheless as really alive to his own interests, as is the master, whom he serves. He has the same animal wants, is born with the same natural desires and necessities, which are absolutely essential to his support and protection. Self-interest is the most important and the absolutely indispensable ground-work of all the acquirements of the master and his dog. The dog must be made to enjoy the display of his talents, by hopes of encouragement or reward, else he will be slow to obey and difficult to instruct.

If you wish your favorite to arouse you at any particular hour of the morning, the hour should be definitely fixed on. If he be fed at that time *only*, it will greatly facilitate his memory and absolutely ensure his punctual attendance. The master should regularly call his dog to the door of his sleeping apartment, at the time required, and give him some very palatable refreshment; after which he should be gently ordered away. This treatment should be continued, until the student be constantly found at his post without being called. On the master's calling, the bed-room door should be left open for several times, so that the animal may clearly understand where he is to go; after which it may be closed and his visit awaited inside. Should he fail to attend at the usual hour, he should be called and the door closed, so that he may knock or scratch for admission. This of course must be repeated according to the aptness of the pupil.

If, after this he should be at his post, and make no importunate efforts at the door, he should be called from the inside, which will excite him to attempt a forcible entry. By repeating this a few times, if you fail to call him, he will get impatient and knock at the door. Be very careful to be mild in your commands, when you order him down stairs, or he might otherwise be led to conclude that he was forbidden to come up. Give him his fee, pat, flatter and gently dismiss him. If you please, you may cause him to lie on a mat, outside your chamber till you are ready to go down, when you should take him out of doors and exercise him in a little frolic, &c. This would be an extra inducement to his regular attendance.

TO MAKE TRUSTY WATCH DOGS AND GOOD RATTERS.

Barking is the peculiar prerogative of Dogdom. By many, an animal that makes an incessant yelping, disturbing his master and annoying his neighbors, is considered a *first rate* watch dog. This is certainly a false criterion : a baseless conclusion. An animal that is really good, will not be annoyed by the distant yelling of ill-bred mongrels, neither will he be excited by every form that crosses within his gaze, nor will he exercise his voice unless he have some cause of suspecting a trespass on his domain.

When a dog barks without sufficient cause, he should invariably be checked. Should he persist in making unnecessary noises of any kind, you should wait concealed, somewhere near him, so as to catch him in the act, and punish him accordingly, to the tune of "*In, Sir.*" A few light and timely corrections will suffice to silence him, and impose on him a salutary dread of your presence, and should he occasionally forget himself, a simple "*In Sir*" will take a wonderful effect on him. On the other hand, he should be excited to vigilance in the right direction, and should be praised in all lawful efforts to ward off the attacks of the invader. He should have the extent of his range clearly pointed out to him, and be also discouraged in any attempt to pass the boundaries of his stewardship. It is well to walk round the premises with him occasionally, and excite him at anything nearing his bounds, at the same time, peremptorily checking him, should he attempt to cross the barrier. He should not be allowed many acquaintances, neither should he be permitted to follow any but his master. A stranger may be employed to strike against the fence, or annoy him at his kennel. Should he appear listless, he should be urged to the attack. A bullock's or horse's head, or a large bone of meat may be given him, when he is chained, and should it fail to render him watchful, a stranger should poke it occasionally with a long pole. He should not however be allowed to gnaw his bone too near, when hungry. A hard bone is very wearing to the teeth of a hungry animal; but I consider it a benefit to a certain extent, if the animal be not too hard set with hunger, to injure his teeth.

If you wish him to seize every stranger he sees, you should make the effigy of a man and encourage him to fly at and tear it, and whilst you hold on to his chain, set him at any individuals who may be willing to second your efforts in making him a "*regular grabber.*" If he have any original *grit*, you may temper his disposition to any grade of severity; either reducing it to a lower standard, by introducing him to society, accustoming him to strangers, keeping him always unchained, checking him in his barks, snaps and growls, feeding him on a farinaceous or vegetable diet, allowing him to accompany a variety of persons, placing him in a situation where there is a great deal of passing; in fine, you may, by constant checks and tyrannous severity subdue his hyena-temperament, till he becomes scared at the rustling of a leaf, or the creak of a shutter. It must then be left to your own judgment, to mould him to your will, to direct, moderate or excite his instinctive and reasoning developements. In the selection of a full grown guard-dog, whose character is already formed, of course, you must be somewhat governed by the position and extent of the premises, to be committed to his charge, and the nature of the services to be required of him. If you prefer raising one from a puppy, I should recommend a Newfoundland, St. Bernard, or a cross between the two, as calculated to make the best family-dogs, which from being generally admired by every one and less liable to ill-usage, are noble and frank in their deportment, free from treachery, less ferocious, yet more powerful and imposing than canines of minor growth.

They are in the habit of holding without tearing, watching without yelping, and with a slight knowledge of the world, readily distinguishing the man of business from the sneaking beggar, welcoming legitimate visitors, yet denying admission to suspicious invaders.

In spite of all risk and trouble, I decidedly prefer raising my own dog, as I then know *exactly* what he is. Should he not equal my

KING CHARLES SPANIEL.

KING CHARLES' DOG.

A perfect specimen of Charley hound:
Of all canines the rarest to be found.
His points are eight, yet, if in ought he lack,
Like a base counterfeit, we send him back.
Head, eye and ear, nose, coat, shape, color, size:
In these combined, the stamp of beauty lies.
Head, full and round, large eye, projecting clear,
With short snub nose, and long well feathered
ear;
Ten pounds, or less may be allowed to weigh;
The smaller, the more valuable they say.
Well shaped his form, nor should a hair of
white,
A doubt of his royal pedigree invite;
Of glossy coat, with raven locks beset,
Face, breast and limb of tan, and body jet.
To Second Charles of England, owes his name,
A regal gift from Second Charles of Spain.
Although, since then two hundred years have
flown,
Still fashion's favorite, as when first was known,
He wears his honors, with becoming pride,
Jealous with ought his tribute to divide.
Flattered by all, the menial and the great,
On him the Page and powdered Flunkey wait;
On velvet couch, with Royalty reclines,
And with the queen, and heir presumptive dines.

anticipations, I should attribute it to my own neglect, provided he were the offspring of undoubtedly good stock. There may be exceptions, though it has not hitherto been my misfortune to encounter *one*.

For a good Rat-dog, select either a Scotch or an English Terrier. Scotch is the hardiest and stands the most work. When he is young, give him something he can kill, without being much punished, a small rat on a string, or a mouse. Put him often at a rat hole to scratch. If you can, let him be with an old killer, that he may see the performance. Excite him well, before you let him have the rat. Don't let him pound him much after he is dead, don't hunt him on a full stomach to disgust him with the taste of the rat, nor allow him to kill many at first.

ON THE TRAINING OF FIGHTING DOGS.

As I am particularly requested to compound a chapter on the training of fighting-dogs, for the satisfaction of the curious, I will endeavor to present a few general ideas on the subject, for some of which, I beg to acknowledge my indebtedness to a learned professor of the art. The subject is grating to the ear of most people of refinement, by whom the practice of Dog-fighting is justly condemned as neither respectable nor moral. Simply testing the courage and endurance of particular breeds of animals, (whose valor we are anxious to prove, in order to satisfy ourselves of the intrinsic merits of the stock as guardians, hunters, &c.), may perhaps be pardonable, to a certain extent, as these virtues are important ingredients in the component parts of a trustworthy companion and defender; but that an animal, whose pluck has been thoroughly verified, should be teased, torn and tortured, solely to satisfy the depraved taste of the thoughtless and desperate. few would dare to assert. However strange it may appear, the owner of a fighting-dog is perhaps as careful and tender over him, as the lady with her parlor-pet. The slightest insult offered to his dog would be a personal challenge to himself, and although the animal may be devoted by his guardian to battle and death, the poor confiding brute is greedy of the honor of perishing in defence of him, who sacrifices his only disinterested friend, to reap the benefit of his sufferings and the glory of his scars.

These dogs (Bulls and Bull-terriers) are decidedly the most courageous, but not naturally more quarrelsome than others; but no sooner can they run, than their latent passions are excited and their courage put to the test; they are perhaps secluded from respectable associates at the end of a four foot-chain, there to be aggravated, poked and worried by their owners and others, through whose instrumentality they are defamed, dreaded and despised.

A dog, to be in good fettle and condition for

fighting, must not be allowed to carry more flesh than is necessary for his health, and that should be firm and solid. When he is matched to fight at a certain weight or under, he has generally to be reduced or increased in weight; more commonly the former. In either case, at the commencement of his training, the animal should be (what is technically termed), *purged out.* His stomach must be first cleansed by about two grains of Tartar emetic. On the following day, he should have small doses of castor-oil or other opening medicine, every two or three hours, until his bowels are thoroughly purified. When this is effected, the renovation, by care, regular bracing exercise and diet, begins. The food should be of the most nourishing kind, yet great care must be taken not to overload the stomach. He must be fed lightly three times a day, so that he may be enabled to stand the repeated and arduous exercises to which he must be subjected, as his endurance has to be tested by as much hard work, as he can bear. Good beef, broiled and very little blood left in it, should be his diet, with hard biscuit occasionally, or his diet may be varied if occasion require. No blood, raw meat, liver or vegetables may be given him. The quantity given him must depend on his appetite, his condition, and the amount of flesh to be worked off by exercise. He should be allowed very little water ; at the same time, fever from thirst should be carefully guarded against; therefore he may have little and often, that he may require the less. He should be kept in a sufficiently warm temperature, and not exposed to either cold or heat. Should he be taken out in the cold air, his loins should be covered, and he must be kept moving at a brisk pace. He had better not be exercised out of doors, either in hot or cold weather, excepting early in the morning in summer. As to the ways in which he may be exercised, they are various : the harder the work in reason, the better. A stuffed bag may be suspended from the cieling, and when the dog is muzzled, he should be excited to seize it. A large ball may be rolled for him to run after, or he may run a few miles occasionally at a brisk pace, following a horse. These exercises must be persisted in as far as he can conveniently bear, which must be left to the judgment of his trainer, but the animal should never be allowed to exhaust himself too much at once, or to suffer for want of food or water. If his bowels should become too constipated, a little magnesia may be given him, perhaps an injection of soap suds, or his exercise may be increased. If he should be in anywise relaxed, his beef should be more cooked, his biscuit more baked and his exercise diminished for a season. However no powerful purgative should be given, unless in case of an absolute stoppage. While it is highly important that he should not be overfed, he must not be reduced below his strength. As a safeguard against a mistake of this kind, he should be weighed every morning before feeding. His best fighting and most healthy weight should be ascertained, as it is safer to give one's adversary the advantage of a pound or two than to reduce one's dog below his real fighting standard. The less your dog has been accustomed to exercise, the more time should you demand previous to his fighting; as courage without endurance is a common defect in dogs, who have not been thoroughly hardened to toil; and many a plucky animal has turned for want of breath, when he had courage enough to face a hundred deaths. In hasty matches, dogs are often rapidly sweated down, which is very disadvantageous to them and ought to be avoided. The amount of food ought not to be much shortened too suddenly, but a little more or less every meal. After hard exercise the animal should be well rubbed and well covered.

COMPARATIVE VIRTUES OF POINTER AND SETTER.

MUCH has been said with regard to the respective merits of Pointer and Setter. Some Sportsmen stoutly mantain that the Pointer is far the superior, whilst others aver that the Setter is greatly to be preferred. Each however, has his distinctive merits. He, who has been the owner of a few good Pointers, and has chanced to be the proprietor of a bad Setter or two, is inclined to believe that the Setter must be the inferior, and vice versa.

This is a wholesale mistake, yet by no means a common yet unfair inference. The Setter is hardier, stands his work better in cold weather, is generally superior as a water-dog, bolder in thick cover and less suspectible to injury by thorns, &c. The Pointer stands the heat bet-

BLENHEIM SPANIEL.

BLENHEIM SPANIEL.

Of Charley stock, in shape and feature par,
If nought contend his regal stamp to mar;
Orange and white, the genuine it is said,
Or black and white, with features tinged with red.
Descended from an ancient Spanish race,
In vain, his prime original we trace;
Once a famed hunter, of Castilian state,
Tho' since enfeebled and effeminate;
So elegant, so highly bred and so genteel,
These honored traits his pedigree reveal;
His virtuous failings, that once vice were deemed,
His passive dignity, now most esteemed.
If ought of preference 'twixt the two be found,
Yield it in favor of the Charley hound;
The latter fuller tasselled, more compact,
With larger eye and feature more exact.
I've oft' remarked, with beasts of every grade,
Hardier and healthier is the darker shade;
This in a measure may perchance explain,
Why Charley more of vigor may retain.
As Charley's virtues are of Blenheim true,
It bodes me not his merits to review;
If further scrutiny, your thoughts engage,
Please turn to Charley, on the other page.

ter, can travel farther without water, is considered less difficult to break and less headstrong in the field. The one suffers more from the cold, the other from the heat. A Setter appears to forget his training more easily than a Pointer; the only way in which I can account for it, is the mixture of Spaniel to which I believe the former is partly indebted for his origin. If either can boast of originality of race, I should certainly, (contrary to the general opinion) attribute it to the Pointer, who shows no trace of Spaniel, and cannot have inherited his bird-hunting and *stationary* instinct from the Foxhound, from whom he is said by Naturalists to have descended. To the Setter appears to belong the stubborn wildness of the Spaniel. The Pointer if not delicately reared or too finely bred, will stand on the average as much work as the Setter.

The color of a hunting dog is of some little importance. Dark colors absorb the rays of the sun much more than light ones, and are consequently less adapted for hot climates. In hot weather, the Pointer may be said to be preferable to the Setter on account of the lightness of his dress, although the sun itself would take more effect on the thin-coated Pointer, than on the thicker covering of the Setter whereas the air, which would keep a Pointer cool, would scarcely be felt through the heavy dress of the Setter.

Before we decide then, which is to be preferred, the Pointer or Setter, let us take into consideration Breed, Habits, Climate, Weather, Country, &c., and stake our opinions accordingly.

TRAINING AND BREAKING POINTERS AND SETTERS.

I AM not aware that there is anything mysterious in the art of training a Sporting-Dog; although it might be inferred from the scarcity of thoroughly broken animals, either that it were a secret, revealed only to a few professional Breakers, or that few ever made the attempt, either from lack of time, talent or self confidence. This may be sufficient to form a plausible reason for neglecting the education of the Sporting-Dog; though, after all, to come when he is called, and to do as he is bid, is about all that the most scrupulous could *exact* from him; the balance must be left to develop itself in his own native instinct and sagacity. It necessarily follows that an early education is of the highest importance. It is then that his habits are formed, his powers developed and his submission secured. Should he not b introduced to his fielding or training, till he has nearly reached his growth, he *can* be *broken*, it is true, but with far greater difficulty, and at the risk of annihilating the noblest qualities of his nature. He will be always more or less difficult of restraint and will require pretty constant exercise to remind him of his duty; whereas, with an early and judicious course of moderate instruction and implicit obedience, he is well brought up, and when more fully developed, requires but a slight introduction into any new field of labor, to arouse his already well organized intellect.

Breaking is certainly a very appropriate term for pounding bad habits out of canine pelts; habits, which never could have been contracted, had ordinary attention been paid to early tuition. When animals commence their training after months of entire freedom from restraint, severity is often necessary, as they become so naturally self-willed, as absolutely to require *Breaking*. It is the easiest thing in the world to prevent a bad habit, but often next to an impossibility to restrain it.

It is a common old Proverb "It's hard to teach an old dog new tricks." but hard indeed as it is, it has continually to be done, yet is often done so imperfectly, and I may add so improperly, that a well-trained dog is an exception, to the army of half-broken ones; so that sportsmen are continually in trouble, for want of a first-rate dog. One is too wild; another isn't staunch; a third won't fetch his game; the fourth isn't under good command; the fifth pounds his bird; the sixth won't take the water; the seventh bolts at the first scolding; the eighth is apt to take after rabbits and squirrels; the ninth won't point the dead bird; the tenth is often inclined to disobedience or may follow another Sportsman, who may offer him a bait. I could enlarge on the defects of many *nominally broken dogs*, but fear I may be accused of doing so already. I enumerate these vices, simply to repeat, that were they early taught and brought up to habits of implicit obedience, these failings would seldom or never occur.

In the first place, if you wish to raise a Sporting Dog, get two; so that if one should die, you may still have one left. If one be better than the other, keep the best; if they be both good, one will pay the other's debts, if you feel inclined to dispose of him; though I decidedly recommend you to keep them both. See that they are the offspring of good and healthful stock. If you have the choice of a pup, select the strongest, the boldest, the handsomest of the litter. Nothing like a little fire to work upon. "The wildest colt generally makes the best horse." As to color, it is mere fancy, and in my opinion amounts to nothing, except in as far as climate is concerned, or the color of the ground you may be called to shoot over. I do not imagine for a moment that the dog himself is the better for being either white, black, orange or liver, but a light color is certainly preferable in a hot climate, as the sun has less effect on it. I refer you to several of the preceding "Dog Tricks," which will assist you in training a Sporting Dog, as well as any other breed, such as: "*Down, seek and find, fetch and carry, going in the water, going on, keeping in, &c.*."

This is all very well, but a Sporting Dog, requires somewhat more than this; he must be trained to hunt, must be practiced in finding his game, quartering his ground, &c., he will require continual restraint and must be kept within reasonable distance of his master. If he only be well bred, he will need but little excitement to attend to his work. His natural instincts will only require directing or restraining to suit his master's will. His habits of implicit obedience may be formed either in or out of the field, but he should be brought to practice as early as possible in the theatre of his glory.

There are only two points to be attended to in Dog-training, these are: first, what the animal shall be compelled not to do, and secondly, what he shall be taught and induced to do. The first point is far more easily overcome than the second, and simply consists in decided checks on all his attempts, either to enforce his own will or to act in defiance of that of his master. The second requires somewhat more of knowledge, judgment, insight, patience and discretion than the first. It consists in moderating and directing his natural powers, engaging them to be subservient to your will, and in moulding them to act well the part they are destined to perform.

Let us suppose him then, perfectly *up to the mark* of Down charge! Come in! Keep in! Hie on! Seek and find, fetch, carry, go in the water! (according to previous lessons), or at any rate perfectly obedient, as far as he has been taught. We will now teach him, or rather let him show us how to find the game, &c. By way of trial, suppose we get a live quail or partridge, clip its wing, attach a string to its leg and let it run a hundred yards or so in different directions, to test his nose, (a dead bird may be dragged along, if a live one cannot be obtained). Select a good sized field, drag it, or let it run in four different directions, set the dog on the scent, so that if he go wrong, you may direct and encourage him to hunt *in* the right direction. When you finish dragging, put the bird in a box and test the actions of your dog, making him Steady, &c., as he approaches it. Where game is abundant, of course this sham hunt need not often be resorted to, although a few minutes may occasionally be found for practice at home, when there is no spare time even for a short shooting-trip. "Down charge" may be taught to be obeyed by the discharge of the gun, if the report be often made to accompany

MASTIFF.

MASTIFF.

Serious and stern, majestic, brave and bold,
The Baron's pride, in Halcyon days of old,
Escutcheoned oft, by knights and men of state
The dreaded guardian of the castle gate.
His head, somewhat the contour of the Bull,
With pendant ear, deep chest, both broad and
full :
In color red, or tawny, by the by,
Deep hanging jowl, black lip, and threatening
eye :
His coat close set, and shoulder doubly strong,
From tip to tip, he may be six feet long.
By massive walls and ponderous bars confined,
Alone, he reigns, contented and resigned ;
Heedless of danger, marks no distant sound,
Solemn and pensive, stalks his dreary round :
The thief's detector, and the foeman's dread,
Silent and listful, notes each stealthy tread ;
Honest, ingenuous, true in all his ways,
Emblem of safety, in the bygone days.
Let not degenerate stock his name disgrace,
Nor soil the virtues of this noble race ;
Dauntless of yore, and just as sturdy now,
He bears the stamp of England on his brow ;
Earnest in friendship, and of candor full,
Distant to strangers, like a true John Bull.

the command, but many have a great objection to it, as the dog may be often checked in his duty, by the discharge of another fowling piece. This may be left however, to the option of the owner. Quartering the ground is not difficult to teach, but requires considerable good humor and encouragement, accompanied by "*Hie on*" and the wave of the hand in the required direction. Should he take the wrong beat, he should at first be recalled and redirected, and thus continually exercised in following the voice, accompanied by the wave of the hand, so that he may be eventually commanded and directed by the hand alone. Various methods are adopted by Breakers to teach dogs to obey their commands. I have seen many a poor animal with his neck in wounds by the use of the force collar, (a strap lined inside with spikes, or a string of spiked balls) to punish the poor beast, upon every light deviation from his master's command. A long string is attached to the collar, and the check is given when any order is not immediately executed This method, I certainly do not admire, although there are cases (where animals have been entirely neglected in early life), which may absolutely warrant it, when all milder attempts have proved fruitless.

Another method is adopted to prevent a dog from pounding his game. He is taught to fetch and carry that only, which will hurt his mouth, if he press hardly on it. But the difficulty in teaching a dog to fetch is greatly increased, when he is continually suspicious of injuring himself; therefore if this method be adopted, great care must be taken that the article used for fetching purposes be so fixed, as in no way to injure his mouth except upon hard pressure. A better and safer method however, I believe to be, to accustom him to carry a partridge or quail, teaching him by suitable instruction, reprimand and correction, that he must neither mumble, maim, nor mutilate it. He will not be found to fetch as cheerfully, of his own free will, if his gums have suffered by the trial. Nevertheless the spiking system, if carefully carried out and without severity may occasionally be advisable in perverse subjects, when the disposition to pound appears difficult to eradicate.

The principal error committed in training Sporting-dogs, is in the use of severe and threatening language not unfrequently accompanied by the lash, to induce the animals to perform an act, which they cannot thoroughly comprehend. Now, when a dog is caught in an act of positive transgression, punishment may serve to convince him of the wrong committed; but on the other hand, an act of *non-committal* is not so easily defined, and the correction may often be interpreted by the sufferer, as a caution against its performance. Therefore encouragement, rather than threats should be the basis of all our attempts to direct the instinctive developments of the sporting-dog; our rebukes and punishments should be reserved for enforcing submission, and of testifying our disapproval of conscious disobedience. Every thing should be done to ensure both respect and affection, and severity will seldom be called for. Recipes for training dogs will be of little service, unless their owners have common sense enough to comprehend somewhat of the varied dispositions of canine nature. Some animals need to be dealt very gently with, whilst others are almost insensible to moderate treatment, yet firmness without severity, determination softened by patience, must be our general rule

The exceptions must be managed, according to the judgment of the trainer.

The amount of reprimand and correction required in such hard cases should however be dealt out in graduated doses, so that, at all events *enough* may suffice. The Sporting-dog, especially should have a few minutes run every day, not only for the benefit of his health, but to prevent his wildness in the field. Dogs, after being tied up for a length of time, become so elated, when set at liberty, that they are not only excessively wild and often unruly, but unfitted for a day's work and apt to wear themselves out in a hurry ; whereas a dog, regularly exercised, is seldom known to tire, is always in good condition, easily kept under good command and rarely troubled with sore feet. Many sportsmen are in the habit of letting fly a charge of dust-shot at their dogs, when they undertake to run after the game, or when they refuse to obey call. In France, especially, I have seen many peppered sterns. It may have a good effect sometimes, (if our animals could only get used to it) but I consider it a very dangerous practice, as I have known several dogs utterly ruined by it.

An old and well-trained dog is very advantageous in assisting in the field-training of the young beginner; though the latter should be previously well versed in all necessary acts of obedience and submission, or it will generally render him the wilder and interfere with the tactics of the more experienced. If the young dog you are training, give evident proofs of a lack of *nose*, or game-scenting powers, you had better dispose of him at once, as this is a defect, for which no virtue can ever atone. It is well to carry a few crackers in your game-bag and give your dog a bite now and then, to enliven his spirits and increase his endurance. Give him but little meat, during the working season, unless it be well boiled and mixed with Indian meal, oat meal or cracker, &c., whichever be most convenient or suit him best; but, if you can get nothing but meat, don't keep him too short, on that account, as his strength must be kept up. A good rubbing, a good supper, and a warm bed will do him good after a hard day's work.

GENERAL REMARKS ON THE DIS EASES OF DOGS.

It may perhaps somewhat surprise those who have hitherto been accustomed to a variety of incomprehensible Latin Prescriptions, receipted to cure Diseases which are not positively known to exist, or which are so mystified by anatomical technicalities, that they cannot be easily recognized by the uninitiated. Yea: I doubt not some of my readers may be astonished, (on reading my simple remarks and practical instructions on the Diseases of Dogs,) that I have neither unvailed the secret of the Apothecaries' shop, nor dissected every fibre of the canine fabric. These things, I have carefully avoided, first, because I am by profession neither Chemist nor Anatomist; secondly, because my object is to simplify that which is too often rendered unintelligible, and to present a condensed list of antidotes, rather than a profusion of infallible cures. I perfectly agree with my learned friend *Deschamps*, who acknowledges the existence of only one Disease, "a *Disorganization of Nature*," and one cure, "the *Reorganization*" I will proceed still farther by stating my belief that Nature effects through suitable relaxation and gentle stimulants far more than can be forced on Her by drastic purges or powerful astringents. Preventives generally indicate cures; upon this impression I have based my ideas and am satisfied in having carried them out in my treatment of the Diseases of Dogs. If I err, I am convinced it is on the safe side. I have nothing to say in contradiction to the opinions of others, but as that which I offer is the result of my own experience, I have reason to hope it may be tested, before it is condemned. As, in a certain sense, all Diseases are one, I have not particularized *every ailment* incident to the canine fraternity, but simply those, which may be identified by the non-professional, understood by the inexeperienced, and relieved without medical advice.

PUCK.

BULL-DOG

BULL-DOG.

Sullen, morose, unsociable and grim!
Show me the man, who'd dream of trusting him!
With short snub nose, full, treach'rous glaring eye,
Projecting teeth, small ear and forehead high;
Capacious chest, with muscle, well displayed,
The Boxer's bully, and the Tinker's jade;
For them he fights, the scars alone his prize,
True to the last, for them, unpitied dies.
Exposed his vices, now his merits scan;
The latter real, the former due to man.
By nature true, courageous, serious, stern;
Excited oft, his latent passions burn;
Rude urchins, educated in the street,
Rowdies genteel, who on the corners meet;
Some men of sense and title too, in fine,
Make cruel pastime of this brave Canine.
Concealed to view, and worried, day by day,
Trained to the Bait, the Battle and the Fray,
Inured to hardship, 'reft of every friend,
His life's a torment, and a boon his end.
Tho' few his social virtues dare to boast,
Yet those who know him best, will prize him most;
While others yap, and yelp and yell, and fly,
Carve o'er his grave; "I conquer or I die."

DISEASES OF DOGS.

FITS.

ALL breeds of dogs are more or less subject to Fits, although among the coarse mongrel kinds, they are but little known. Dogs of fine stock, of tender constitutions, those glutted with rich food and lacking necessary exercise are its most common victims. I consider fits to originate in the lack of a regular circulation of the blood, or from an overcharged digestion, perhaps more than from any other cause. A weak-nerved dog, who is much confined in the yard or house is over joyed at the chance of an unlimited romp, and becomes so highly elated as to cause an extra flow of blood to the head, causing a temporary pressure on the brain, thereby rendering the sufferer wholly unconscious even of the presence of his master. This

I believe to be one cause. Another is a disorganized digestion, (more or less deranging every part of the system), striving to vent itself by forcible efforts to expel an overflow of vitiated humors. A third cause is an exposure to the sun, acting more immediately on the nerves of the brain. Fits are often confounded with Distemper, of which they are ofttimes a dangerous accompaniment. Distemper-fits are quite of a different character to those of which we are now speaking. In all my experience and experiments, I have hit on no antidote or sovereign cure for these uncertain ebullitions of subverted Nature. I will first speak of preventives, before I propose a method of cure. Animals that are subject to fits should be allowed plenty of exercise (within certain limits), and should be fed on light fare. They should not be exposed to the sun, and great attention should be paid to their bowels, which never should be constipated. They should never be fed to the full, nor on any indigestible food. Wet feet will suddenly bring on fits, especially in dogs who have been long confined. I have often noticed how soon these fits were brought on by their feet suddenly coming in contact with cold water. If a dog subject to fits be too fat, his flesh should be immediately reduced by light purgations, his diet changed, whilst he is gradually habituated to an increase of exercise. He should be ridded of every thing tending to annoy him ; he should not be exposed to any excitement, and should he appear to be more joyous than usual, he should be immediately checked, stilled or chained. By noticing this, he may generally be spared the trial. I am speaking now of fits, where no distemper exists, as distemper-fits require a somewhat different treatment. Heated rooms are very productive of these attacks, especially where the creature is allowed to lay under a hot stove. Basking in the sun will often bring them on. Dogs are very apt to get bewildered by the sun, and I have often had to remove them from their dangerous fascination. However, with dogs who have no predisposition to fits, I imagine there is not much to be feared from their spontaneous baskings. The antidotes then are light fare, regular exercise, freedom from excitement, healthy stools, avoiding the hot sun, wet feet, &c. In the majority of cases, previous to a fit, the dog has a wild staring expression, and appears to be somewhat alarmed at every thing he sees ; he will sometimes stagger and run backwards and forwards without an object ; he may then perhaps stand still, his vision and brain evidently wandering ; he may start in any direction before he falls, or he may occasionally fall, without any previous indications, He will often make the most distressing yelping, both before and during the paroxysm, whilst at other times he will be comparatively noiseless, except from the champing of his jaws, from which he ejects a slimy froth.

Thousands of poor brutes (only temporarily deranged), have been destroyed for being guilty of Hydrophobia, although it bears but a very slight resemblance to Fits. Ordinary Fits are very sudden, give but short (if any) notice of their approach and the animal either speedily returns to his consciousness or expires. A sullen, morose, unsociable change may be the forerunner of Madness, but previous to a Fit, the sufferer is generally more profuse and urgent in his professions of friendship. The owner of an animal who is subject to Fits, should always be prepared with a chain and collar, whenever he takes him out, as he can then the more readily secure him and manage him without difficulty. He will thus avoid having him slaughtered, under the popular hue and cry of "Mad Dog."

Although the snapping, foaming, staggering, kicking, yelping, should not be mistaken for Hydrophobia, yet I would particularly advise all those who may be treating a patient in this condition, to avoid being bitten; for two simple reasons. First. The bite of a dog in perfect health conveys with it a certain amount of poison, exactly in proportion to the state of the system, upon which the impression is made. Secondly. Great caution is required to avoid the bite of an animal in this stultified condition, and I am further perfectly satisfied, that his bite under such circumstances would be more likely to prove serious, on account of his disordered state; although there need certainly be no ground for alarm or apprehensions of Hydrophobia. Still as dog-bites under any circumstances are far from agreeable, and furthermore, as the beast is then unconscious of his actions, and especially ungovernable in his jaws, his dental operations should be carefully avoided. He may be safely held by the back of the neck, or kept at a respectful distance by means of a chain and collar; or should he be too powerful to manage in this way, he may be made fast to the first convenient hold. With sluts, Fits often prove fatal to Breeding, either by unfitting the animal for healthy propagation, or destroying the embryo. From such I recommend you to avoid breeding, both dogs and sluts. I would also, advise all owners of confirmed *uncurable fitters* (if such there be), to administer a dose of Strychnine, to stay all further proceedings.

The cure must be somewhat similar to the preventive, with a few simple additions. When he is first attacked, pour a stream of cold water on his head, and immediately put him in a dark place, (or cover his eyes). Give him an emetic of common salt, as much as he can swallow at once. The next day, administer small doses of castor-oil, every two hours, until his bowels are thoroughly, though gently purified. Bleeding may occasionally be resorted to. A little blood may be taken from the ears or tail; a fly blister may be placed on top of the head, or a seton introduced in the back of the neck. Should these fits be found to proceed from worms, the above treatment need not be followed. The worm medicine should be first administered, where you have any doubt about the case. Should worms be the cause, some of the preventives proposed, would be powerless, though certainly not injurious. I have found rubbing to be very effectual in restoring them, when they have been apparently stiffened out for death. A little brandy and water, (say one fifth best French brandy), sweetened, and a teaspoonful more or less, administered every half hour, is often of essential service. Nothing, however, should be given during the convulsive action of the fit, or until the animal can swallow with ease.

DISTEMPER, DIARRHŒA, CONSTIPATION, STOPPAGE.

"DISTEMPER" is a term, with which well nigh every owner of a dog, is perfectly intimate, but the exact source, cause or origin of the disease appears to have baffled the most profound researches of the "*Dogographer*" and the Anatomist, to have puzzled the public at large and completely mystified the *knowing ones*. Nevertheless, a thousand *infallible* cures are receipted for it, the majority of which are admirably calculated, either to hurry a suffering canine out of a miserable existence or render him a cripple for life. Distemper may be attributed to a variety of causes. Like fevers, measles and small pox, it may be considered both infectious and contagious, yet, is still oftener a spontaneous outburst of disease, origi-

BULL TERRIER.

BULL TERRIER.

In him, the Terrier and the Bull we trace,
Well known to all, his famed, tho' compound
race ;
The sluggish Bull-dog, thus, new vigor gains,
The Terrier too, the former's pluck retains ;
Thus stubborn courage and deliberate nerve,
To check the hasty and impetuous serve.
A Mongrel true, yet, tho' a Cur he be,
If right his stamp, no better hound than he ;
Defies the water, braves the very fire,
Unites the merits of his Dam and Sire.
To fix his size or color, were a jest,
Yet true it is, the smallest sells the best ;
A doubtful title, but which some concede
To ought that bears a shadow of the breed ;
Of colors all, weight forty pounds to three,
Too dwarfish for an honest pedigree.
Apt as a scholar, faithful as a friend.
Well armed and ready, valiant to defend ;
He knows no danger, and he fears no foe,
And if vindictive, man has made him so ;
His instinct ever, on his duty set ;
True Courage never was a Bully yet.
Should any doubt, if this be true or not,
Peruse the writings of Sir Walter Scott.

nating in the system itself; yet from what particular influences, has not yet been satisfactorily determined. No antidote or safeguard against its attacks has yet been brought to light, neither has any sovereign remedy been effectual, in averting its fatality. The malady presents itself in such varied forms and types, that it is often not recognized as Distemper, even by those who have had some experience in Dog-keeping; whilst other and widely different ailments are often attributed to Distemper. Its appearance is not confined to any age, season or climate, neither is it peculiar to any breed, or the result of any particular kind of diet, locality or management. One breed is as subject to it as another, yet certainly not equally liable to become its victims. The worthless mongrel stands a far better chance of recovery than the appreciated pet or the high bred Sporting-dog. The reasons of this to me are evident. The cur is hardier, from his cross-breed and habits of exposure, and is naturally of a stronger constitution, consequently, the better fitted to resist disease; is seldom pampered and gorged, gets more exercise and less physic. High bred dogs are always somewhat difficult to rear. There appears to lack in them a certain vigor of constitution, in which the cur is seldom deficient. For this reason, great care is requisite in the raising of choice breeds, till they attain their growth, or pass the ordeal of Distemper. It must not be supposed however, that all dogs must of necessity have the disease, any more than all children are bound to have the Small-pox or Scarlet fever. Again, some have it so lightly, that it is scarcely perceived, whilst others make short work of it, and snuff out in a canter, in spite of all efforts to save. The common symptoms are restlessness, heaviness, disinclination to move, redness and sometimes great paleness of the eye, whiteness of the gums, running at the eyes and nose, loss of appetite, looseness of the bowels, dryness and dirty appearance of the nostrils, dry cough, wasting of the flesh and general debility. Ulcers will often appear about the lips and gums, the breath becomes offensive, and the evacuations have a putrid odor. These indications do not appear at once, nor in all animals, neither can Distemper always be traced, when some of these symptoms are apparent. After all, the general appearance of the patient is more to be relied on than any one of these distemper-like appearances. A marked difference will be perceived in the general deportment of the canine, which any observer of his general habits will not be at a loss to interpret. His owner should be in the habit of keeping a strict watch on him, now and then for a few minutes, without engaging the animal's attention; as dogs, like men, are prone to wear a merry countenance, when the system is diseased. It is therefore necessary to scan their spontaneous movements, which is the plan I invariably adopt in discovering the most important of canine ailments. Of course their various parts may be likewise examined, in order to ascertain the very spot, where any disorganization may more visibly develop itself. Distemper appears to be more fatal at some periods than at others, without reference to any particular season of the year. I have however found it more fatal in the fall of the year than at any other season, especially on the first appearance of cold weather. It may attack a litter of puppies, some very lightly, some severely and others fatally, yet these have breathed the same air, eaten of the same food, occupied the same bed and received the same treatment. Who then shall prescribe an antidote against its inroads, or an absolute remedy against its fatality? Its effects nevertheless may in most cases be greatly mitigated by constant attention to the health of our charge, forbidding the least indisposition to pass unnoticed, and by resorting (as occasion may require) either to gentle aperients, wholesome astringents, or moderate abstinence. I am averse to administering Calomel to dogs. It is decidedly dangerous, and thousands of poor animals have been sacrificed by it: it can only be given with comparative safety, where the animal would be subjected to no kind of atmospheric change, and this would be very difficult to avoid, as his coat cannot be conveniently thickened to suit the weather.

When a whitish mucus fluid runs from the nose, it is almost invariably a sign of distemper. This may be generally considered a favorable symptom, and far more favorable, than a dry hot nose, emitting little or no moisture; in which case I have often found the disease settled on parts more vital and more difficult of relief. I beg of you not to consider Distem

ENGLISH TERRIER, (Black & Tan.)

ENGLISH TERRIER, (Black & Tan).

Of varied color, fashion black and tan,
In England, (say they,) this famed race began,
Red, white, and yellow have been highly prized,
Though sundry tints, by man are oft' devised.
Well shaped his form, with Greyhound-tapering head,
Leg, breast and jowl, well flushed with tannish red;
His body black, with coat, high glossed and fine,
Varying in weight, from twenty pounds, to nine.
If ought of white his feet or breast disgrace,
Too light a red or brindle there we trace;
Too clumsy limb, too coarse his tail or coat,
Doubtful his Sire; his purity remote.
Staunch and courageous, daring in his ways,
Quick as a flash, the noisome rat he slays;
His stern endurance oft' has proved him fit
To slaughter hundreds in the gaming pit.
Of late contrivance, springs a dwarfish race,
Fitted alone the drawing room to grace;
Of tender growth, yet elegant in limb,
Active and sprightly, vigilant and trim,
Watchful alarmist, docile, apt and small,
Is now Yclept the favorite of all,
And oft' reveals the wealth and taste of man,
The perfect, pencilled, tiny Black and tan.

per, this running at the nose, as a simple disease of the mucus membranes. The origin is not there; it is a general attack on the whole system, commonly originating in the stomach. Nevertheless this running ought to be encouraged, by often sponging off with lukewarm water, especially when it cakes around the nostrils, after which a little sweet oil may be rubbed on them. This appears to have but little to do with the cure of the disease itself, yet it is a great relief to the animal, facilitating his breathing, and consequently diminishing his sufferings, thus in a measure enabling him the better to withstand the malady. The principal object in Distemper (as with many other diseases) is to keep the bowels in a proper state, by preventing the system becoming too debilitated to outgrow its attacks. The seat of Distemper being principally in the digestive organs, the stomach must be the principal object of our solicitude. The food should be nourishing, yet easy of digestion; a little should be given at a time, say three or more times per day, according to the strength of the patient, but not to interfere with the operation of medicine. Exposure to wet, cold, or damp is very much against recovery, likewise too much heat or close confinement. A little exercise is beneficial, but this need not be forced. As I have just observed, presuming the seat of the disease to be in the stomach and bowels, let us attempt a cure by first cleansing and thoroughly ridding them of all purulent offensive matter, which I have found to exist in all distempered dogs. This must not be effected by too powerful means, as Nature is more injured than benefited by drastic purges, and often disabled in her efforts to recruit herself. Avoid then strong doses. At the outset of the disorder however, an emetic must be resorted to, to cleanse the stomach. Common table salt will have the desired effect. One good throatful, or as much as can be gulped down at once is generally sufficient to produce vomiting, and should be the dose for any dog, of any size. You need not be alarmed at the quantity, as it will almost invariably be rejected, when given in large doses; or will sometimes act, both as an emetic and purgative, in which case no other aperient will be required for the time being.

I propose then to cleanse the stomach the first

day and give no other medicine. Take care that the patient have plenty of cold fresh water to drink, light fare, beef soup, with rice or pilot bread well boiled in it. or according to the dog's mode of living, with more or less of meat, but well cooked and well mixed. so that it be not eaten alone. Where there is a tendency to looseness. raw flour may be tied up in a fine cloth and boiled for three or four hours, after which it may be mixed in with the soup. It is not so common for dogs with Distemper to be constipated in their bowels; the reverse is generally the case. and has particularly to be guarded against, after the system has been thoroughly cleansed. In many distemper-cases, the dog has a ravenous appetite and appears to decrease in size, according to the amount of food eaten. clearly proving that it passes off undigested, thus leaving the multitudinous parts of the system wholly unprovided for, and the whole frame to wither away. The second day castor oil in very small doses should be administered every two hours, till it operates freely, say, from a quarter of a tea-spoon to half a table-spoonful at a time, according to the age and size of the animal. Should he be very costive, the doses may be doubled. The less medicine given in Distemper, the better, nevertheless what is necessary, must be done. Sufficient warmth, perfect cleanliness,freedom from damp, light diet, and a comfortable bed are essential to a fair prospect of recovery. The strength must be kept up as much as possible, by feeding little and often, but never as much as the dog would eat. You need not be uneasy about his dying of starvation ; he is the last animal in the world to dream of committing suicide. If he will only eat a little, he need not be forced, except on particular occasions, such as his absolutely refusing all manner of food for a day or two, in which case a little strong beef soup may be fed to him with a spoon every hour or so. Fits are very common to dogs with Distemper, and still more common to those who have it not. As an accompaniment to Distemper, they are far more dangerous ; but let us once see the digestive organs right and all the dependencies will follow suit. In wounds and local attacks, local applications may in a measure suffice, but in distemper, the righting of the whole machine must be effected at the main spring. For distemper-looseness,

SCOTCH TERRIER.

SCOTCH TERRIER.

Small, rough and whiskery, and of sandy hue
Though sometimes gray, and oft' of dusky blue;
Clear, bright, inquisitive, sagacious eye,
Moustachiod lip, with brows deep shaded by;
Brave, hardy, vigilant and ever gay,
First famed on Scotia's lofty hills, they say;
Kills fox and weasel, skunk, racoon and cat,
Rabbit or squirrel, hedgehog, mouse or rat;
Onward he rushes, with impetuous ire,
His wiry pelt dares bramble, bush and briar;
Through matted brakes, he threads his thorny way,
Digs in the earth, or tempts the flood for prey;
Not swift of limb, the fleeter game to trace,
Attacks the foe, within his hiding place;
Of noxious vermin rids the house and store—
Inspects each corner, searches every floor;
When cunning Renard, pressed by boisterous hounds,
Rushes to earth and thus the pack confounds,
The valiant Scot assails him in his den,
All gore-begrimmed, he drags him forth again.
His coarse exterior, some may chance contemn,
Others his blunt expression may condemn;
Yet none his virtues ever dare deny;
His merits rigid scrutiny defy.

diarrhœa or dysentery, the best remedy I have found is 4th proof French Brandy, ground allspice and brown sugar, viz: a gill of French Brandy, a table-spoonful of ground allspice, and a heaped table-spoon of brown sugar. Mix the allspice and sugar in a saucer and stir in the brandy. Place this saucer and its contents on an inverted saucer, and set fire to the ingredients, and stir gently till the fire goes out. When cool enough, pour into a bottle, shaking it well, every time you pour off. Give the patient from half a tea-spoon to half a table-spoonful in twice or three times the quantity of water, every hour or two, till the looseness is checked. If the animal should be at anytime too costive, give small doses of castor oil as before recommended. With these simple remedies, the enemy may be kept at bay, and Dame Nature will have a fair chance of minding her own business. In a healthy dog the nose is cool and moist, and is consequently a very fair index to the general health; although when the animal is consumptive, or much reduced in flesh, the nose, ears and extremities are all cold, from a lack of the power of general circulation. Small stimulative doses are then very useful; a little weak, well-sugared brandy and water, every hour or two, with or without strong beef tea, according to necessity. Looseness is far more dangerous than costiveness, and far more difficult to arrest on a sure basis, as it should by no means be too suddenly checked by powerful astringents. The brandy and allspice compound before recommended, I consider to be the safest and most efficient. With this I have not only cured the most obstinate cases of Diarrhœa, but have restored animals, who appeared to have breathed their last. I once sharpened my knife to skin a favorite King Charles' Spaniel whom I supposed to be breathing his last, but suddenly changing my mind, I gave him three doses of this compound, at intervals of half an hour. After the first, he kicked out his hind leg, after the second he slightly raised his head; after the third he tottered off several yards, and from that hour rapidly recovered. Remember, I am a powerful advocate of little and often, in all cases of prostration from disease, more especially in Distemper. Nature in an exhausted state is paralyzed by powerful doses, whilst she appropriates advantageously the gentle droppings. If stoppage should not yield to small hourly doses of castor oil, the bowels may be well rubbed, with brandy spirits of turpentine, or alcohol with spirits of camphor and ether. An injection of blood-warm soap-suds may be used and repeated every fifteen minutes till an operation is effected. Should this not succeed (and the patient be not inconveniently large), give him a bath, as hot as he can readily bear it, for five or ten minutes; after which, rub him heartily and thoroughly dry; keep him well covered, till he has entirely recovered its effects and a natural reaction has taken place. I have however, very rarely failed with small doses of castor-oil, which I have occasionally persevered in for thirty-six hours. Of course on the first indication of relief, it must be stopped and small doses of light nourishing food be substituted. When the distempered dog shows heaviness about the eyes or giddiness, he should not be exposed to much light. As what effects the eye, effects the brain and what effects the brain acts on the whole system. A slight affection of the brain, requires in a dog, but little outer excitement to produce fits, which tendency should be checked, as much as possible.

Fine bred pets are very easily unnerved, especially when in a delicate state of health ; quietness is as essential to their recovery as to a human being in a similar condition. Do not presume that all fits have any connexion with distemper. They often arise from a naturally weak and nervous temperament, and oftener still from indigestion and worms. The latter may generally be known by a tightness of the belly, (especially in puppies), irregularity of stool, sometimes loose and sometimes the reverse, jumping during sleep, a rumbling noise in the inside ; by the animal dragging himself along on his hind parts, by his suddenly yelping and changing his position, and by the oft renewal of his yelling. These symptoms have seldom anything to do with Distemper, though they may sometimes co-exist with it. The worms should be got rid of first and Distemper afterwards, should both be visibly marked together. Worms, in young puppies are often mistaken for Distemper. The looseness arising from worms should not be checked, till the worms are expelled by medicine. Stoppage is also caused by worms, by solid knots of them blockading the intestines. As the worm medicines I recommend under the head of "*Worms*," are not calculated to injure the constitution of the most delicate, it may be safely administered whenever worms are suspected. Dogs have been inoculated for Distemper, but I have not heard of any benefits arising from it. In raising Sporting-Dogs, my plan is to introduce them to the disease, when they are in a healthy state, but not when the disease has assumed a virulent form, I think the most favorable time to be just after they have finished shedding their teeth. They are then generally in a healthy condition, and on that account the disease seldom proves fatal; to say nothing of our being fully prepared to treat our patients accordingly. It is very rare indeed for an animal to contract the disease twice, though it may often return, if it has not been judiciously or thoroughly eradicated. I would advise those then, who would raise Pointers or Setters, to force them into Distemper at a suitable period, as it is more particularly trying to lose a sporting-dog, after the trouble and expense of raising and breaking; to which may be added the blighting of our long cherished hopes of an invaluable field companion; but on no account expose him to the Disease. till he present his new set of teeth. as they are often totally ruined by its effects; not only the organs of mastication, but his breath, his health and his beauty. Setters, Pointers, Greyhounds and Newfoundlands are more severely affected by Distemper, than the ordinary breeds of Dogs. Their food in early life should not be too gross, neither should the stomach be overcharged; for although, as I have before observed, there be no antidote against Distemper, yet its attacks may be mitigated by attending to the general health of our favorites. We must first be careful to procure healthy stock, keep them on wholesome food, neither stuff nor starve them, keep their ears warm, their noses cool, and their gums rosy; neither compel them to be hot or cold, wet or exposed.

In Distemper, the matting up of the eyes should be cautiously guarded against; by often washing with warm milk and rubbing a little sweet oil on the lids. When the animal cannot see, his trouble is heightened, and the whole nervous system thereby affected, and as dogs are very sensible and sensitive animals, endowed with almost human intellect, we must remember that whatever tends to cheer and enliven them, has a happy effect on their physical ailments. When the heaviness of the head is not relieved by aperient medicines, the crown of the head may be shaved and a fly-blister placed thereon; a little blood may be taken from the ears, or the head may be often bathed with cold water and carefully dried off. However, I do not recommend bleeding, except in extreme cases. Instead of a seton, so much recommended by Dogologists, I prefer passing a sharp red-hot iron about the size of a lead pencil through the skin at the back of the neck, leaving the wound to fester; it often has a happy effect, in relieving the head and carrying off the humors. It may be allowed to heal of its own accord and reopened, if requisite. If any twitching or shaking of the limbs should come on, it should be immediately taken in hand, and every means used to keep up the circulation, by rubbing in a strong liniment, composed of spirits of turpentine, alcohol, oil and laudanum, or if nothing be used, the friction alone will be serviceable. "Butler's Mange Liniment" has been used with great effect, in such cases. In this state, especially, the animal should not be exposed to any kind of damp; the bowels should be kept in a proper state, the food should be light, he should be carefully supplied with fresh water and a comfortable bed. If the weather be favorable, he should have as much exercise as he can conveniently bear. These nervous twitchings, if not attended to in time, are difficult to cure, and even with all our precautions and attentions, are always to be dreaded. When they neither yield to care, medicine, diet or friction, the poor sufferer had better be put out of his misery. I have had valuable patients lying helpless, for many months, long after the whole hind parts were completely paralyzed and lifeless, and have at last been induced to destroy them by drowning, the only method of proving whether their limbs might ever regain their motion, in the agonies of dissolution; but the sufferers have invariably sunk, *unweighted* to the bottom. Light twitchings happen to dogs occasionally, when they have no Distemper, and often depart without help. For this I have found nothing so good as rubbing and warmth. Mange and other cutaneous eruptions are considered by some writers as forerunners of Distemper. Distempered animals often have postules on the bowels principally, but they have not the appearance of ordinary mange. When these postules break out in Distemper, it is far from a favorable symptom. They should be treated however, as Mange, and great care should be taken of the sick one, as he is then more liable to take cold, than at any other period. Distemper is more apt to be fatal with animals fed on a rank meat diet, but do not suppose that any food is an absolute preventive; I have seen hundreds die, who never tasted anything but cracker and milk, and many indeed, who never lived long enough to *eat* anything at all. Dogs are very rarely blinded by Distemper; the bluish film which often covers the eye, naturally disappears, as the animal recovers, and it is far better let alone, with the exception of gently washing with warm milk and water. If a dog be taken with Distemper, he should be removed from his companions, to avoid infection, though I have found this to be no positive guarantee, as the causes originating it in the one, may equally operate on another, and Distemper may be lurking in the system for weeks, before it makes a decided appearance. I could enumerate a host of Distemper remedies, but as my object is to simplify, I shall not enlarge on their respective virtues.

MANGE

Next to Distemper, Mange is the most common and the most troublesome disease, that Dog dom is heir to. No breed, no age, no size is exempt from its attacks. It is propagated in a variety of ways, and is to a great extent hereditary. It is also contagious, is spontaneously produced by gross feeding and dirty bedding, and is sometimes an appendage to Dis temper. I have seen puppies, covered with Mange sores on their entering the world, entailed on them by their Sire or Dam, or perhaps even of origin more remote. A dog, by simply lying where a diseased animal has been, may become contaminated, or by coming in contact with him in the street. Fortunately, it cannot be taken by any human being, (at least I have never known a case), any more than the Scarlet Fever can be conveyed to a dog. It is very similar to the Itch, in the human race, and I should think surpassed even the genuine "*Scotch Fiddle.*" I have good grounds for believing that ordinary Mange, is produced by insects, generated in the blood and brought to life on the skin. Of the secret of their formation, I confess my entire ignorance; but as outward applications are far more efficacious than anything taken internally, and as one rubbing with the Mange-Liniment allays the irritation, I am still further convinced of its being an animal production. Are not insects visibly brought to light in the same way on the surface of the human body? The tendency of the secretions of the system to produce these animalculæ may certainly in a great measure be averted, by keeping the body in a healthy state, so as to check any stagnancy of the juices, which favors the spontaneous production of animal life. Wholesome and moderate fare, exercise and cleanliness are the grand preventives, "Butler's Mange Liniment and Flea Exterminator" is a sovereign cure, as it not only eradicates the disease, but speedily reproduces a superabundance of hair. But I would recommend both preventives and cure. As the Disease is principally caused by impurities, perfect cleanliness must be attended to without, and all grossness avoided within, where there is any indication of eruption. If "Butler's Mange Liniment" cannot be had, Oil of Vitriol, diluted to the strength at which it can just be borne on the tongue, without burning, to which add a quarter of an ounce of finely ground Indigo and a quarter of an ounce of Gunpowder, (mixed well together), to a quart of the diluted Oil of Vitriol. The animal should be first well washed (if the weather, &c., be favorable), and then rubbed all over with the mixture, every other day. Every alternate day, he should be well anointed with common fish-oil. An ointment of Sulphur and Lard is another remedy, but I object to Sulphur, as it often strikes to the limbs of the animal, injuring him for life, so if this be used, he should be carefully kept from taking cold. It is preferable that he should be washed, before every application. Whatever be used, the beast should be rubbed from the tip of the nose to all his extremities and the mixture must be well rubbed in. "Butler's Mange Liniment," never fails to produce a beautiful coat and to allay the irritation on the first application; which I have never known any other compound to effect. Its application should however, be repeated every other day, for three or four times, to ensure death to all forthcoming animalculæ. No animal occasionally rubbed with it, has been known to take the Mange, and for beautifying the coat and cleansing the skin, its equal is not to be found. Dogs affected with any cutaneous eruption, should be subjected to a thorough but gentle physicing, and their mode of living should be entirely changed, in order to give the constitution a fair chance to purify itself, and put a stop to all further spontaneous insectile productions among the sluggish secretions of a disordered frame

The visible symptoms of Mange are, bare spots, irritation, eruptions on the skin, a shortening, or unnatural falling off of the hair, redness on the back, bowels or other parts. Fleas also produce a kind of Mange, perhaps the most difficult of cure; as they disease and poison the whole surface of the body, and if neglected sometimes reduce the system to unrecoverable weakness, by depriving the dog of his necessary rest. Very old dogs are the most difficult to cure, but I have not met with an incurable subject yet. The disease, however, should be taken in hand as early as possible, as, to say the least of it, it greatly annoys and disfigures the sufferer for a season.

RABIES, HYDROPHOBIA.

It is somewhat difficult to define the varied symptoms of Hydrophobia. Incautiously to attempt it might perhaps arouse fears, where there existed no cause for alarm. For the consolation of the nervous however, I may commence by assuring them, that a mad dog is indeed a very rare production, and that perhaps not over one in a thousand of those accused of it may be pronounced guilty. Every ill-bred street-roving bone-grubber, every dog despairingly seeking his master, every canine in a fit, every poor beast, overcome with heat and fatigue, every affrighted quadruped seeking refuge from his merciless pursuers, in fine, every favorite, who may portray a certain strangeness of demeanor, must of course be mad. In the last ten years, I have not had a single case

ESQUIMAUX DOG.

ESQUIMAUX DOG.

Pet of the Laplander and Esquimaux,
Where dwarfish men and stunted mosses grow ;
Where winter long extends his dreary reign,
And ponderous icebergs choke the northern
main.
Fox-like in shape, nor varies much in size,
Short ear erect, sharp nose and cunning eyes ;
Or black or white with coarse and lengthy hair ;
Condensed by climate and by scanty fare ;
Thick bushy tail, flat on his back and curled ;
Tho' in the hour of peril, oft' unfurled ;
Lively and active, vigilant and gay,
Not lacking courage, anxious to obey ;
Spitz, Pomeranian, Arctic, Esquimaux,
By various epithets, the breed we know ;
Yet so peculiar is the genuine race,
The least impurity his traits deface ;
His compact form, thick set, robust and trim,
His sprightly gait, black nose and supple limb,
His dress unique, his dark inquiring eye,
All base ignoble counterfeits defy.
In German States, where men most need their
wits,
Is most esteemed of all, the watchful Spitz ;
A bribeless guard, not oft' with strangers free,
There's many a hound, that well a Spitz might be.

of Hydrophobia, among an average stock of sixty or seventy dogs, under my own eye, nor a solitary case, among some twenty or thirty more, kept for me by others; although I have had many, which, had they fallen under public notice, would no doubt have excited the usual and alarming echo of Mad dog! Mad dog!

A vacant, wild, sullen expression of the eye, movements to and fro, apparently without an object, a tendency in the animal to devour that, which he would at other times have left unnoticed; unusual indications of affection, in which he persists, in spite of his master's commands: a marked uneasiness in all his movements; a constant changing from place to place: a disposition to snap on the slightest approach of annoyance: a desire to retire from the presence of any one: an unwillingness to quit his retreat or to come at his master's call, licking his own urine, &c., these are symptoms of Hydrophobia. Yet all these may exist in different animals, and not one of them be bordering on madness, Nevertheless, there is after all, a certain something, in the appearance of an animal with the symptoms of Rabies, that should not be misunderstood by him, who has been accustomed to scan the ordinary movements of his favorite. The decided change which has taken place should not be carelessly disregarded, and when ever any suspicious indications present them selves, the animal should be securely chained or confined, where he may be out of the reach of everybody, until the case be clearly defined. I do not mean by this, that a suspected individual, who has already become the subject of a marked change of demeanor, should be even trusted with his master's fingers, but that he should be collared and chained in such a way, as to annihilate all risk of injury. The eye will generally denote the disposition; therefore where suspicion exists, and before the hand be extended to touch the animal, he should be playfully spoken to by his master, who may gently and jocosely present him some object attached to the end of a long stick, which will be a fair way of testing his feelings.

He should be excited by his usual watch words, that he may afford an opportunity of noting his actions. His usual food and water should be cautiously placed within his reach; in fine, every precaution should be observed.

for although cases of Hydrophobia are happily rare, the bare idea of it, (as an old lady justly remarked,) is no joking matter. Thus, should there be nothing amiss, a great deal of uneasiness may be avoided. Some of the causes of Madness in dogs, I have found to be the following; exposure to the sun, without the power of retreat; deprivation of water, especially during warm weather; unwholesome food, remaining undigested in the stomach; heat, excitement and lack of nourishment, accompanied by continued worryings, peltings, and drivings; the constant wear and tear of the whole nervous system, produced by fleas being allowed to accumulate; the bite of rabid dogs or venomous reptiles; bones or any foreign object stuck in the jaw or throat. But a more ordinary impulse to Rabies than any of the foregoing, I believe to be the dogged determination of the male in pursuit of the female, more especially when great heat, lack of food and water, and protracted journeyings are added to the torments of unsatisfied lust. Of this I have known several unmistakeable instances; indeed every circumstance attending these headstrong peregrinations combines to agitate and disorder the whole nervous fabric of the naturally excitable canine. Some years ago, I had three cas s of decided madness; two caused by the bite of venomous reptiles; the third by a sunstroke. Of course I safely and securely chained all the patients, and marked their daily progress. The two bitten subjects grew worse and worse, till I relieved them by a merciful death; the third, by my throwing cold water on her, three or four times a day and keeping her in the cool shade, with little light, gradually recovered, and afterwards produced several litters of puppies, one of which lived just long enough to be swallowed by an alligator on the banks of the Mississippi. Neither of these dogs refused to drink, but the two former had lost all power of swallowing, for some time previous to my destroying them. Rabies, caused by venomous bites or objects sticking in the throat or jaws is perhaps the most incurable, as it is by no means advisable for the inexperienced to risk an operation, at an advanced stage of the inflammation. I believe many cures might be effected, if the animals were only kept safely bound in the shade and constantly cooled with water, I mean where

ARCTIC SLED DOG.

ARCTIC SLED DOG.

A noted member of the frigid zone,
Hardy and tough, adapted to his home,
To him the traits of horse and hound belong;
His feats the theme of many a polar song.
Of wolfish form. yet somewhat stouter grown,
The sled dog, sole in Arctic regions known;
With stiffened ear erect, keen prowling eye,
Sharp pointed nose, and coat of varied dye;
His dress compounded of a woolly wire,
Defying cold. disdaining sun or fire:
In vigor strong, to hardship e'er inured,
From pampered taste and indolence secured;
Of lasting foot, with firm and nervous tread,
Unwearied drags the cumbrous Lapland sled.
Or lightly bounding with the travelers' sleigh,
With gladsome trip, makes seventy miles a day.
Parry, McClintock, Belcher, Ross and Kane,
With thankful lip, record his memoried name;
O'er Greenland snows and ice of Baffin's bay,
Hungry and gaunt, he led the trackless way.
For ever barred the sweets of home to taste,
Triumphant sped them through the frigid waste.
O'er the brave Franklin, raise one grateful sigh!
His faithful dog lies bleached and withered by.

the cause may be indigestion, over-excitement or sunstroke. When an animal has been bitten by another, known to be mad, I consider it undoubtedly the safest method to destroy him; although I have known many dogs, which have never been affected by the bite, whilst others have become its victims.

Dipping in salt water, three times following, each time keeping the patient under till he is nearly exhausted, has been thought to take such an effect on the system, as to annihilate the venomous power. True, I remember a case in England, where two dogs were bitten by a mad dog, within five minutes of each other. One was a Pointer, owned by a great sportsman of my acquaintance, who immediately drove twelve miles to the salt water, and there plunged his favorite almost to death. The other dog remained unnoticed and unattended to. In a few days after, the neglected animal went raving mad and committed fearful ravages, whilst the Pointer never portrayed the most remote symptom of Hydrophobia, during the remaining years of his life. I have also seen various persons at Southampton, almost ducked to death, to avoid the consequence of the bites of mad dogs, and this was considered an all sufficient safeguard. But I am rather slow at hasty inferences, especially on the subject of mad dogs. With regard to the fact of the Pointer mentioned, his system might not have been as susceptible of absorbing the virus as that of his unlucky neighbor, neither might he have been as severely bitten, and as it is well known that all dogs will not be affected by bites of rabid animals, the Pointer might have belonged to the class of non-absorbents. With regard to the persons alluded to, they *might* have been bitten either by an imaginary mad dog, or by one whose nervous system alone was under temporary derangement.

The bites of really mad animals differ widely in their poisoning powers, and in many cases I imagine the danger would be very trifling. The venom issuing from a really corrupt system must differ widely in virulence from that produced by simple nervous excitement. I have often been bitten by dogs, laboring under temporary derangement and mad to all intents and purposes (if animals unconscious of their acts may be termed insane,) and I certainly have never felt any fear and but little inconvenience from it. Bet the bite of a really rabid animal, who has had the disease festering his whole frame, is at all times to be dreaded. Neither the Fits in Distemper, nor ordinary Fits should be mistaken for Hydrophobia. They bear but little resemblance to it. Fits, in rabid animals are preceded by different premonitory symptoms, and are generally the sequel of a train of incoherent, extraordinary and unreasonable performances. In all fits, however, the animal should be handled very cautiously, as his unconsciousness may result in inflicting injury, where none was intended, and bites are at all times more or less poisonous. A person bitten by a mad dog should have the wounded parts immediately taken out by a skilful surgeon, and the sore should be afterwards thoroughly burnt out with lunar caustic. I would also recommend the application of a dozen leeches to the neighboring parts, and a soft poultice to encourage the flow of blood to a limited extent, whilst a bandage be tied above the wound, to lessen the circulation, till the operation be terminated. Cooling aperient medicines cannot be amiss; the treatment however should be regulated through the advice of a skilful practitioner.

From what I have seen and heard, I have some little faith in salt water-ducking, and would certainly try it, as it would not be likely to do any injury. Do not wait for a Doctor to cut out the bite, if he be far off, and you have judgment enough to operate, without cutting an artery, or risking danger in the loss of blood. Time is every thing, and if attended to early, there is very little fear of danger even from the most venomous bite. Many foolish people imagine that if a healthy dog bite a person and the animal should at any after time become rabid, that the individual may on that account become the subject of Hydrophobia. This must be all moonshine. By the same method of reasoning, should the person with whom I associate in New York, die of the yellow fever in New Orleans, I must also fall a victim to it. How many faithful animals have been sacrificed, through this nonsensical idea! Certainly it were better for a dog to suffer death, than that the nerves of any human being should be continually agitated even by such peurile humdrum, yet it is high time that reasoning minds should avoid conclusions, where there is no connection between cause

SCOTCH SHEPHERD DOG.

SHEPHERD DOG.

'T were vain, the Sheep-dog to depict in verse,
In doggerel rhyme, his merits to rehearse;
Known in all regions, by a foreign name,
Distinct his origin, his use the same.
Of varied caste, of different form and size,
But ever honest, vigilant and wise;
On Grampion hills, on Alps or Pyrenee,
A matchless hound, of doubtful pedigree.
Unlike his brethren, born to lounge at ease,
Raised on the mountain, nurtured in the breeze,
The truthful index of his master's eye,
With him alone, content to live and die.
On boundless plain or thickly crowded street,
The faithful Colly, with his troop we meet;
With speaking gesture and expression firm,
Directs each movement, dictates every turn.
Inured to hardship, dreads nor cold nor storm,
The sleepless sentinel, his flock to warn;
Unseen, alone, his midnight watch to keep,
The bribeless guardian of the helpless sheep.
Gentle his sway, yet stern his strict command,
He guides unerringly his fleecy band;
No truant lamb evades his watchful eye,
Nor dares his sovereign generalship defy.

and effect. Hydrophobia signifies a dread of water ; but it is no proof of canine madness that a dog should refuse to drink, neither is it a test of his sanity, should he drink to the full. In a certain stage of Hydrophobia, where the head is the most affected, anything glistening causes the unconscious animal to start and vary his course. When kept in the dark, or with little light, the rabid animal will generally keep secluded and still ; therefore in all cases of affection of the brain, he should be kept as much as possible from the light. Mad dogs when not excited by glaring objects often drink freely to assuage the fever raging within, but in their flighty paroxysms they shun all dazzling objects which flash on their disordered vision.

COLDS, COUGHS, ASTHMA, INFLAMMATION OF THE LUNGS.

Colds and Cough, when unconnected with any other complaints are seldom difficult to cure. Dogs are very liable to take cold, but we seldom notice it, except when we consider it either the forerunner or accompaniment of Distemper, or some serious affection of the lungs. Indeed an ordinary cold, discernible only by a light watery oozing from the eyes or nose, seldom requires any medical treatment, should no other symptoms present themselves. An emetic of common salt, and the next day from half a teaspoon to half a table-spoonful of castor oil, repeated every two hours, till a good operation be effected, keeping the animal in a sufficiently warm place, feeding him rather less than usual, (should he be inclined to fat or not habituated to exercise) will often cure a newly-contracted cough or cold, without further remedies. Should these fail, try the expressed juice of onions, boiled up with sugar; a teaspoonful or so to be given every three or four hours. Rubbing the throat and breast with spirits of Turpentine and oil in equal parts, or "Butler's Mange Liniment," if you have any, will be of service. If the dog will drink fish oil of his own accord, he may have a teaspoon or table-spoonful two or three times a day. A few drops of paregoric, in ten times the quantity of water, administered occasionally, I have also found to afford relief. Distemper-cough, must be treated as a part of Distemper and other symptoms taken into consideration, but in any case, what I here recommend, cannot fail to be of good effect. Blisters may be resorted to, should other means prove unsuccessful, and should there be a continuance of fever, the animal may be bled. I am no advocate of bleeding except in cases of incurable fits; blisters also are very troublesome, and I think may generally be avoided. Small and repeated doses of fish-oil tend greatly to relieve Cough or Cold, but should not be allowed to act too freely.

A warm bed, light fare, freedom from damp or sudden chills must however be particularly attended to.

Asthma is troublesome, and not so easily got rid of. It appears to settle more firmly on the constitution than either cough or cold, and is commonly the result of over-feeding, of continued lack of exercise, of exposure to chills, &c.; therefore asthmatic quadrupeds should be kept on light diet, or if otherwise, should never be fed to the full, be well supplied with fresh water, and not be exposed to cold or wet. Gentle emetics often relieve for a season; rubbing the throat with a powerful liniment, not allowing the patient to get fat; gentle and regular exercise, all contribute to effect a cure. Milk, sweetened with molasses, is good for all complaints of the chest in dogs. Asthma is with difficulty totally eradicated, but, by attending to the remedial means, the animal will generally suffer but little, except in cases of age, or a debilitated constitution. Blisters and bleeding are resorted to by those who understand the business, but their effects are seldom of lasting benefit. Hot baths and hearty rubbings are also very beneficial and the bowels should never be constipated.

Inflammation of the Lungs imparts to the animal a drowsy, sleepy appearance. He is little inclined to lie down, and is continually drooping his head, when sitting on his haunches, is generally very thirsty, with little appetite and hot breath. It is often an accompaniment to Distemper, when it is more fatal than under any other circumstances. When this disease is manifest, the diet should be very light and nourishing; the animal should be kept comfortably warm. From ten to twenty grains of Nitre with from two to five grains of antimonial powder may be given morning and evening. A little croton-oil or blister-ointment may be rubbed on the chest, or a bag of hot hops be placed between the fore legs for a few hours. But after all, care and attention are the most important, as any cold taken by an animal in this state is liable to be fatal. The fœces should be carefully noted, and Diarrhœa or Constipation immediately attended to. Rapid consumption will be the result of Inflammation of the Lungs, it the disease be not attended to in time. Warm baths, if the animal can be afterwards thorough ly well rubbed and dried, will tend to invigorate and increase the circulation, but they should not be often repeated, or they may have the contrary effect.

WORMS

WORMS are very annoying to Dogs of all breeds and ages, but are seldom fatal, after the teething-period. Puppies often come into the world, loaded with worms; if not, they generally begin to suffer from them, before they have left off sucking. In puppies, worms may be detected by an enlargement and tightness of the bowels, a weakness in the eyes, coldness of the ears, a restless movement from place to place, particularly after a meal. Sometimes they produce great pain and cause the animal to start up, continually uttering distressing cries, as though he were suddenly pricked with some pointed instrument. In dogs of maturer growth, the suffering does not appear to be very severe, but the annoyance generally reveals itself, by the animal dragging his hind parts along the ground, when the worms approach the rectum. He will grow lean without any apparent cause, will sometimes be ravenous and at other times refuse his food. Although I believe few full-grown animals fall victims to worms, yet they are a constant source of annoyance and destroy both the comfort and comeliness of the animal. As well nigh all dogs are more or less troubled with them, and as they may be destroyed without resorting to dangerous medicines, the necessary remedies may be applied, where there is suspicion of their presence. In young puppies, sometimes a few small doses of castor-oil will carry them off. Should this however. not suffice, other medicines must be resorted to. There are many excellent remedies for worms. The three following I consider all-sufficient: First, Cowage and Bitter Aloes. Second, finely powdered Glass, followed by a dose of Bitter Aloes the next morning. Steel-filings, followed by a dose of Aloes the next day. Try three successive doses of the first, every other morning on the animal fasting, if no improvement be visible, use the second in the same way, and if that does not give satisfaction, administer the third. Either of them may

POODLE DOG.

POODLE DOG.

White, black or brown, thick clothed in wooly
hair,
A general favorite of the Ladies fair ;
The showman's pet, of mountebanks the boast,
Said to originate on Gallia's coast.
Varies in weight, from sixty pounds to three,
Kind disposition, and from malice free ;
His dress (of course,) must be in fashion worn,
His nose, and back, and feet all neatly shorn.
In courage lacking, yet in fondness true ;
His merits known, his vices hid to view ;
Rendered effeminate, by female care,
By tender petting and from lack of air ;
Cuddled in laps, and nestled warm in bed,
His pampered appetite on dainties fed ;
His race has dwindled ; yet a hardy few
Of vigorous growth, his sterner traits renew ;
Famous in water, vigilant on shore,
In Paris numerous, in Madrid a bore ;
Found in all climates, known to every rank,
The silky Cuban and the curly Frank ;
To music dances, vaults on head or toe,
Barks out the hour, or plays at Domino.
Such are his talents, that ere long, I guess
He'll beat Paul Morphy, into fits at Chess.

be mixed up in fat or suet, which the dog may be tempted to swallow, if the pill be wrapped in a piece of meat; if not, he may be easily made to take it. Rubbing the bowels with spirits of turpentine is very good, but it should be rubbed in, till thoroughly dry. Puppies with worms should be kept warm and comfortable, as when wormy they are weak and chilly. There are a variety of these worms: thread-worms, tape-worms, wire worms, flat-worms. The wire-worm, I have found the most troublesome and fatal; they are an inch or so long, about the size of small twine, very hard, and sharp pointed at both ends. They collect in knots, impeding the passage of the fœces, and will often, if neglected, bore through into the cavity of the bowels, after which the animal will not long survive. I have opened many puppies, where the intestines have contained nothing but worms, proving that what should have nourished the animal had been completely absorbed by them. Cough is sometimes indicative of their presence, consequently may sometimes be relieved by the worm medicines. An emetic of common salt is a good beginning towards their destruction, as they often lodge in the stomach and sometimes creep out at the mouth and even through the nose. If a dog does not gain flesh on a reasonable allowance of food, he may be suspected of worms and treated accordingly

Calomel, of course is a great worm cure, but I never use it, because I consider the remedy worse than the disease.

WORM DOSES.

First.

1-2 ounce Steel-filings, mixed in fat and made into twenty-four pills, one more or less, to be given every morning, according to size of dog.

Second.

Teaspoonful Cowage; 48 grains powdered Aloes; made into 12 pills, one more or less to be given every morning.

Third.

A pinch, more or less of powdered Glass, mixed in suet, each dose.

RHEUMATISM, PALSY, PARALYSIS.

DISEASES of the nerves are not at all uncommon with dogs, and are by no means the most easy of management, as they are often the focus of other maladies, which seem to revenge themselves on the nervous system, and must not be considered mere local affections. They are not however so difficult to cure, if taken to in time, before the muscles become too contracted to admit of restoration. Of course the longer the contraction has existed, the more distant the cure ; therefore all nervous affections should be taken in hand at the earliest stages.

Rheumatic affections in dogs, (as well in as the human race) are more effectually treated by simple preventives, than by any amount of Gamboge, Colocynth, Calomel, &c. The following causes may suggest the most natural remedies, viz: sleeping in the damp, exposure to cold after violent exercise, sudden change from heat to cold, lack of sufficient circulation after coming out of the water, gross feeding, combined with lack of exercise, &c. No doubt the above are amply sufficient to produce any malady, incident to the canine system; still, well nigh every dog is continually exposed to them, yet, how few comparatively are troubled with rheumatic complaints.

To the over kindness or cruel treatment of the master, are to be attributed the majority of these ailments. The Sportsman hastily lays down his gun and hurries to his repast, whilst the poor dog, who has traveled three or four miles to his master's one, is left out of doors, chilled and unattended to, impatiently waiting at the door for a stray bone, or a few indigestible scraps, instead of his having been heartily rubbed, decently fed and comfortably bedded. The house-pet is hurried out from under the hot stove into the cold air, or is perhaps condemned to shiver awhile at the door, to atone for a midemeanor. The favorite Newfoundland is indulged to a bath, and tied up dripping to his kennel; the trusty guard-dog is allowed to bask all day by the fire, and is condemned to bark all night at the moon, to keep himself warm. Continued constipation of the bowels is often productive of various forms of muscular affection, by checking the regular action of the system, and producing an irregular and confined circulation. In fact, anything that tends to disorder the canine fabric may develop its results in a rheumatic form. I hope I may not be accused of Quackery, if I am inclined to treat all diseases more or less alike; but one thing is certain, the stomach and digestive organs are the root of almost every malady, and must be the first objects of our solicitude, in all physical derangements. To many, the idea of giving an animal castor-oil for the Rhematism, or Salt for a broken leg, may appear decidedly preposterous. But with Rheumatism we must also begin by purifying the system and attending to the diet. The patient must be kept as much as possible from sudden changes, must be fed on light, yet nutritious fare, be provided with a comfortable sleeping place and not be allowed to go out in wet weather. In the kennel to which he is chained, all chinks should be stopped, to exclude side-draughts, or he should, (if not in the house), be more properly kept in the stable, or any convenient enclosure. Repeat rubbings, morning and evening of the parts affected with strong penetrating liniments,* keeping the bowels gently open, and occasionally administering the anti-rheumatic compound :

Gamboge,	6 grains,	mix in fat or suet.
Colocynth,	3 grains,	
Bitter Aloes,	1 scruple,	

Divide into six pills, from half a one to two whole pills, to be given every evening, according to the size of the animal, and if necessary, a small dose of castor-oil, to be administered every following morning. After the above amount of pills have been taken, (or six doses), the patient should be allowed to remain two days without medicine, unless it should be requisite, to stay a looseness or promote an evacuation. Setons and blisters may be resorted to, should milder treatment prove abortive, and when there is inflammation, and there be strength enough to warrant bleeding, it may occasionally prove advantageous.

* "Butler's Mange Liniment," is very efficacious.

Warm baths are often productive of great benefit, if the animal be not permitted to take cold. The muscular affections produced by Distemper should be treated in a similar way. When the hind legs become weak or partially paralysed, a common pitch-plaster is excellent. The hair should be thoroughly shaved off, or it will not stick: the animal may be either muzzled, or a little oil of Tar rubbed occasionally on the plaster will generally prevent him from biting it. Strychnine has been used to advantage in desperate cases of Rheumatism, Palsy and Paralysis, and I have known one instance, where a dog was cured by a dose intended to kill him. With all this, if it be used at all, it should be in very minute doses and under the advice of a medical man, and then only as a forlorn hope.

To Calomel, we are indebted for many cases of incurable Rheumatism; therefore avoid it, as much as possible, except in cases, where the sufferer is free from exposure, or where other remedies have failed; even then I would only give about a third of the ordinary veterinary dose, combined with a sufficient quantity of Rhubarb to correct it, and Aloes to carry it off. As in other disorders, strengthening medicines may be necessary, such as Peruvian Bark or Gentian Root mixed with ground Allspice. For delicate dogs a covering may be made to go over the loins, where there is a tendency to weakness, which should be put on only, when he is taken out.

COACH DOG.

COACH DOG.

Denmark ('t is said,) was once the favor'd State.
Where Coach dogs first were wont to congregate;
Now graces every canine catalogue,
The well known spotted coach, or carriage Dog.
Of growth genteel, of Pointer form and weight,
Is highly prized by fancy men of late;
But every spot must be distinct and clear,
Of equal size, and free from blot or smear;
His form erect, with tapering tail and fine
Smooth close-set hair, and perfect every line;
Thin drooping ear, clear-chamber'd glassy eye,
Lest either lacking, should his race belie.
From mean associates, scornfully abstains,
Nor mongrel cur his confidence obtains;
The horse his friend, the stable his delight,
Follows by day, and beds with him at night;
Onward they travel up the hill of life,
Unenvious, sociable, devoid of strife;
Attachment strange, yet true, 'twixt horse and hound;
For 'mongst them all, was ne'er a traitor found,
With joyous glance, salutes his friend at dawn.
And cheers him in his weary journey on;
In days of languor, or whate'er betide,
His faithful guardian, sleepless by his side.

DISEASES OF THE EYE.

THE eye of the Dog is subject to a variety of morbid affections, the majority of which do not originate in the eye itself, but in a disordered state of the secretions; therefore, the general health has to be taken into consideration whilst our efforts are alike directed to the locality. The eye may be inflamed from fever within, may portray the paleness of general debility; may display its sympathy with disease fastened on the whole system, or may be deranged simply from outward causes; yet, in nearly all cases, the foundation of its cure must be in righting the main-spring. Any disordered action of the secretions will generally be visible in the appearance of the eye. Unless the disease be purely local, no powerful wash or lotion whatever, should be used to the eye of the Dog.

Gently washing with lukewarm milk and water, keeping it perfectly free from mucus, rubbing in fresh lard, butter or goose grease around the neighboring parts; add to this light fare, ligh aperients and little sunshine, and you will do more to abate inflammatory action, than by any powerful appiication.

The dull blueish film, often formed on the eye of the distempered animal, requires no application whatever, except that the eye be kept perfectly clean and lightly greased. It generally clears away, if the animal recovers; whether or not, I consider all local attempts at forcing a cure are worse than useless. The film or coating that makes its appearance on the eye of a healthy animal should not be allowed to thicken or increase, or it may eventually terminate in cataract or blindness. White sugar, finely pulverized and blown into the eye through a quill, every morning, will at the outset generally effect a cure. A little butter dissolved in the corner of the eye is often of great service. When the foregoing are unsuccessful, finely powdered alum, in minute quantities blown into the eye may have the desired effect. Should this fail, it may be washed with a weak solution of sugar of lead, or sulphate of zinc, otherwise a solution of nitrate of silver, one grain to a wine-glass of water with a tea-spoonful of brandy in it. Only a drop or two of this must be dropped in the eye morning and evening. Common wounds, bruises, swellings and such like in the region of the eye, are speedily cured by "Butler's Mange Liniment;" but this should never be dropped into the eye. Where this is not to be had, a compound of Brandy, olive oil, laudanum and turpentine may be gently rubbed around but must not be allowed to enter the eye. Where nothing else can be found, goose-grease, lard or butter will be of great service. Cataract in the eye of a dog is seldom cured, if firmly established, as in that state, ordinary applications are of little service, and few understand the operation of removing it; nevertheless, if the patient be of sufficient value, an oculist might operate on it with success, as the animal may be safely and securely bound for the operation.

Running eyes are commonly caused by high feeding, constant colds, lack of general exercise, damp beds, &c. Sometimes they are the result of Distemper and often hereditary, in delicate and high-bred pets. Keeping the eye clean, restricting the animal to moderate fare, allowing him regular exercise, keeping him from sudden chills, forbidding him the hot fire or burning sun are among the principal preventives. This running appears to be a natural leak of the system, and unless the health be attended to, no local application will be availing. I am by profession neither Surgeon nor Oculist, therefore I shall not enlarge on the different affections of the eye, nor infringe on its anatomical technicalities, as I am not writing a medical work, but propose simply to give the results of my own personal experience. For any serious operation on the eye, I would refer my readers to some competent surgeon or oculist, advising them by no means to risk it themselves. If requisite, soft lukewarm poultices of bread and water, bread and milk, flaxseed, &c. may be applied with advantage, where inflammation arises from any cause whatever: as to putting on and keeping them in place, it must be left to the best judgment of the owner of the patient. To keep the eye in a healthy state, especially in animals of high breed and delicate constitutions, everything gross in diet

CHINESE HAIRLESS DOG

CHINESE HAIRLESS DOG.

Of goodly form, oft' portly, plump and round;
In every clime occasionally is found;
Of high repute, in that celestial sphere,
Where dogs are dainties and fat pork is dear.
Called Turkish, South American, Chinese;
Tho' fitted best, John Chinaman to please;
For tastes refined and Epicures decreed,
Good roasted, boiled, fried, stewed or fricasseed;
Guards well the house, and keeps the thief at
bay;
Does useful errands, for the folks by day;
Barks at their pigtails, licks their stunted feet,
And grubs his hasty living in the street;
But woe betide him, when for cooking fit;
It bodes him not, his merit or his wit;
Doomed to the oven, or frying-pan his lot,
His grave the stewpan, or his tomb the pot.
Doubtless well known, in ancient days was he,
Ages before the Anno Domini;
They say Confucius fared on Canine stew,
And sent Pythagoras a chop or two.
Be't as it may, yet dare not raise a laugh,
Such menial hounds inspire no epitaph;
They crave for food, that they may fat the
faster,
And die a sacrifice to feed their master.

should be forbidden, and constipation carefully avoided. Although in many cases, weakness and running of the eyes are incurable, the foregoing preventives will be far more effective than all that medical treatment could ensure. Sleeping in a damp place is highly favorable to the production of overflowing humors of the eye, and no cure can be expected, where an animal given to weeping, is thus exposed. Bleeding and blistering are sometimes resorted to, for redness and other inflammatory symptoms of the eye, but as few of the unprofessional understand these operations, I shall not recommend them here. Some dogs have naturally a ferocious redness about the ball or in the corner of the eye. When this is constitutional, there are little hopes of a cure. In cases of continued inflammation of the eye, a red hot iron, about the size of a common lead pencil, may be pressed through the skin, at the back of the head, (should other remedies fail) and the wound may be kept open, until a marked improvement or a cure be effected.

DISEASES OF THE EAR.

Disease of the ear is mostly confined to over fed animals. Wandering mongrels and dogs boarding at their own expense are not so liable to outbursts of gross humors. Heavy-coated dogs are oftener attacked with it, than the less thickly-coated. Regular exercise, cleanliness and simple diet are the most important preventives. The ear is subject to disease in a variety of forms; common inflammation, sores, boils, ulcers, canker, polypus, &c. Any ailment of the ear may generally be discovered by the animal's shaking his head and rubbing it with his paw. Should there be any thick or matted hair inside the ear, it should be cleared out as gently as possible, with a pair of tweezers or the thumb and finger. Whatever be the form of the sore, the ear should first undergo a thorough cleansing twice a day with Castile soap and lukewarm water for two or three days, without any other application. After every washing, the ear should be rubbed perfectly dry. After this, a weak solution of alum may be used twice a day, gradually increasing its strength for three or four days in succession; after which rub in "Butler's Mange Liniment," which never fails to heal up any kind of wound or sore. If this however be not at hand, make an embrocation, composed of one-fourth spirits of turpentine, one-fourth oil of tar, and a half of olive oil well mixed together, which, should be applied every day. If the ear should be very thick and much inflamed, a soft poultice may be applied, either of flaxseed meal, bread, or Indian meal made with strong green tea. But, if we can do without poultices, so much the better, as they are troublesome things, and most animals dislike bandaging. It may occasionally be advisable to lance a sore, should it continue to inflame, after other applications have proved unavailing, but should it form a natural head, I have found it better to allow it to take its course and burst of its own accord. With solid tumors, the case is different, if they fail to diminish from the use of ordinary means, the only remedy is to have them carefully cut out by a skillful practioner. Whatever be used as a wash for the ear, it should be bloodwarm, both on account of its being more suitable to the sore or inflammation, but far less shocking to the animal. A weak solution of extract of lead, with one-tenth brandy may be used as a wash, and if used bloodwarm, may be poured into the ear, if the part affected cannot be reached with a sponge. For obstinate diseases of the ear, that yield neither to a purification of the system, nor to ordinary outward applications, the base of the ear may be bored with a red-hot iron, about the size of a common lead pencil and the wound kept open till the disease is stayed. I have found this to be of great benefit: it acts as a counter-irritation and thus relieves the affected part. The edges of the ears are subject to a scabby mangy appearance, which destroys the growth of the hair, and sometimes gradually inflames the whole flap. "Butler's Mange Liniment" will speedily cure this. If it cannot be had, rub the ear every two days with mercurial ointment, and every other day it should be thoroughly cleansed and washed off with alcohol, as strong as the animal can bear it. If a violent discharge of the ear should not be checked by the foregoing remedies, the ulcer may be burnt out with caustic. Often a putrid odor will issue from the diseased ear, though this cannot continue long, when it is kept thoroughly clean. A solution of chloride of lime, very weak, will act as a purifier. This should be used with the sponge, if the diseased parts can be reached. In curing diseases of the ear, as with all other ailments, the most important thing is to attend to the general health of the patient, as otherwise the disease may be only driven from one locality, to be forced out of another. It may be often necessary to muzzle the animal, on applying the wash, poultice, seton, &c.; he may easily be kept steady and harmless, and should on no account be neglected, on account of his aversion to handling, but as little roughness as possible should be resorted to. Thorns should be carefully extracted from the ear, before any inflammation sets in, as they then become more difficult to detect and more painful to extract. I recommend as a preventive against sore ears, that they be kept perfectly clean by a regular systematic cleansing with soap and water. I really believe filth to be the groundwork of half the diseases of the ear, as, however clean other parts of the body may be, the ear is generally left in a dirty condition. Few even, who wash their little pets ever think of thoroughly cleansing the inside of the ear.

SPRAINS. DISLOCATIONS, FRACTURES, WOUNDS, SWELLINGS IN THE NECK AND THROAT.

Sprains.—Growing dogs, in particular, from their wild reckless gambols are very apt to sprain their joints. I have had a number of cases, where a puppy has become lame for a considerable time, yet the exact nature of the sprain could not be defined, as nothing could be felt out of place. I have therefore been led to suppose that some of the small tendons uniting the joint were over-strained. If not attended to early, a constant lameness may be he result. The rubbing in of a strong liniment such as "Butler's Mange Liniment," or any other powerful counter-irritant, bathing the part often with cold water, enforcing on the animal perfect rest, administering cooling medicine should there be any sign of inflammation are about the best means of effecting a restoration.

DISLOCATION, or the displacement of a joint, should be immediately sought for, should there be the least suspicion of its existence; as a joint remaining unset for a time, not only becomes difficult to re-set, but serious inflammation may arise, from its being neglected, and the cure be rendered exceedingly difficult. By carefully feeling for the joint and moving the limb gently backwards and forwards, a dislocation may be easily detected, and little skill will be required in setting; but don't pull too hard at once; let your efforts be graduated, according to necessity, or you may strain the nerves in righting the bones. After all is made right, the same means may be used as those recommended for Sprains.

FRACTURES demand more skill in their treatment, as the bones require to be set in their place, and small pieces may have sometimes to be extracted. The splinters (two thin pieces of wood, whalebone or cardboard) should be carefully put on and bandaged over with a strip of calico, under an inch in breadth, but great cau-

TURNSPIT DOG.

TURNSPIT DOG.

Yellow or brown, with muzzle often black,
Low bandy legs, and disproportioned back;
Eye of intelligence, ear rather small,
Nose quite extensive, teeth, the best of all;
Short coat, stout built, inelegant in form,
Problem unsolved, where Turnspit first was
born;
His home the kitchen, 'prenticed to the cook,
He notes her movements, scans her every look.
When fat and lazy, and for work unfit,
Is oft' *incog.*, when called to turn the spit;
Hides in the garret, or would fain be lame,
So dinner's late, and Bandy gets the blame.
Defends his post beside the kitchen fire;
Nor stranger dare provoke his latent ire;
Displays his ivories, and with angry tone,
Growls out menacingly, "let me alone."
Unlike his compeers, never made a pet,
Confined at home, and at his duties set,
His working time p'raps three scant hours a
day,
From them, unguarded, slyly steals away.
Although his master often may you greet,
Ashamed t' acknowledge Bandy in the street:
Alone perchance you'll find him on the jog,
The awkward, crooklegged, fireside kitchen
dog.

tion must be used, not to tighthen them too much, which would produce inflammation ; yet they must at the same time be made fast enough, to prevent them slipping, or causing a disunion of the bones. It should not be taken off until the fracture be thoroughly and stoutly knit, unless there should be appearance of inflammation. The dog should be kept at rest, until sufficiently recovered, and then he should for a season be led on the chain, and not be allowed to romp at discretion. The fracture may be afterwards daily strengthened by penetrating liniments, and cold water applications. Fractures, other than of the limbs, will require skilful treatment, or must be left to work their own cure. Dogs are wonderful creatures and really recover the most desperate poundings, without medical advice or surgical aid; therefore, what you don't understand, you had better let alone.

WOUNDS are seldom difficult of cure, and will heal up without our assistance, unless the system be disordered ; in which case, cooling medicines may be necessary to purify the blood and facilitate the efforts of Nature. If a wound be large, it should be sewed up with thread; by uniting the parts, it will heal the sooner. Oil of Tar and olive-oil in equal parts will both cleanse and heal a wound. "Butler's Mange Liniment" is also a speedy cure. Any kind of grease is soothing, but should have no salt in it, unless the wound be foul, in which case it may be washed occasionally with weak alum water, which is very cleansing and prevents the formation of proud flesh. For mange sores, use "Butler's liniment." In any case, keep the animal cool and quiet; provide him with light food, fresh water and comfortable lodgings.

SWELLINGS IN THE NECK AND THROAT will sometimes make their appearance, so unexpected and suddenly, that we are at a loss to account for their origin. With external swellings, I have seldom found any difficulty. Spirits of turpentine, oil of Tar and olive-oil in equal parts form an excellent liniment, which should be well rubbed in morning and evening. Should lancing be necessary, it should be done by some one that understands it, and this not till the inflammation has pretty well reached its height. Cooling medicines may be necessary to purge the system and lessen the tendency to putrefaction in the humors. Any strong liniment will be of service, and if none can be had, bathing the part in cold water may effect a cure, or if you will tie the animal up in a cool place, feed him light, give him a regular supply of fresh water and a little cooling medicine, a cure will generally be effected. Nature, with a little encouragement knows well how to reject impurities, that have been forced upon her. Should the swelling arise through any foreign object having poisoned the part, every effort should be made to extruct it: if this cannot be effected, linseed-meal with a little oil of Tar may be used as a poultice, or a pitch-plaster with a hole in the centre be placed over the part. When the swelling is inside the mouth or in the throat, it becomes more serious and difficult of management, as when there is irritation or pain inside the mouth, a dog gets restless and is sometimes difficult to handle, without endangering one's fingers. Blisters and liniments may, however, be applied to the neighboring parts. Objects stuck in the throat should be pushed down with the first suitable thing that may present itself, as, if the animal be choking there is no time to be lost. A pliable twig, a teaspoon, or table-spoon will answer the purpose; a piece of whalebone will do better. For any settled ailment of the throat, an occasional emetic of common salt will generally greatly relieve the suffering, by cleansing the diseased part, ridding it of purulent matter and perhaps bursting the sore. But with all swellings in the interior of the mouth and neck, I recommend the animal's being safely chained, as he will sometimes becomes exceedingly irritable; so much so, as not to produce Hydrophobia, but such a nervous timidity (I presume) that he dreads the approach of any one, and is willing to attack anything, in apparent self-defence. I have seen several cases of this kind, where my advice has been luckily attended to, thus avoiding any amount of alarm, if not of decided danger. For all disorders of the neck, throat, &c., the bowels should be kept in a proper state, the diet should be light, and the dog should be kept as quiet as possible. When he is unable to eat solid food, he should be supplied with soup, milk, &c. A tea spoon of olive-oil, now and then will afford the throat some relief, as well as impart nourishment to the animal.

PUG-DOG.

PUG-DOG.

Black nose, with body brown and curly tail,
Old fashion Pug! Come tell us whence you
hail!
Thy race declines, thy former history fades,
Tho' once the idol of forlorn old maids.
And t' were as well; thy compact form displays
Far nobler traits than speak thy meaner ways;
Pugnacious front, round head and daring eye,
Thy bumps renowned Phrenologists defy.
With noisy yelp, both friend and foe he hails,
But briskly flies, when ought of pluck assails;
Growls at the moon, and starts at every crack,
And at the sound of danger, turns his back.
Doubtful his pedigree, his origin obtuse,
'Tis clear he's more for ornament than use;
Yet still, with all his faults, there surely is
Something unique about his matchless phiz.
He must have thought how men could be such
brutes,
To pluck his hearing organs by the roots;
A fancy notion, say they, of the man,
A Hollander, who brought him from Japan.
Companion of the gentler sex alone,
'Tis thought that hence he might have timid
grown;
If true it be that "manners make the man,"
What makes the Pug? let him decide who can.

SORE FEET.

HUNTING dogs especially are frequently subject to sore feet. The causes are: traveling far on the hot ground or on a gravelly soil, over work, frost, mange eruptions, improper feeding, &c., but the most prominent of all, is lack of regular exercise. Any human being, unaccustomed either to riding or walking, will feel the sore effects of a prolonged pedestrian or equestrian exercise. Therefore the greatest preventive against sore feet is regular daily exercise. My experience in this is confirmed by multitudes of professional Sportsmen.

The remedies are various. Sometimes simply washing the feet with alum water will effect a speedy cure. Whatever be the application, the feet must first be thoroughly cleansed, and be well protected against dust, dirt, otherwise the cure must naturally be delayed. or the evil increased. A few days rest on clean straw and the application of fresh lard, two or three times a day may be sufficient, should the feet be simply cracked with the heat. If the hair be falling off and eruptions appear, "Butler's Mange Liniment" will effect a cure. If it proceed from a general grossness through the whole system, the diet should be light, and gentle aperient medicines will be of service. A flaxseed poultice is excellent, where there is inflammation. The feet should be carefully washed with Castile soap and luke-warm water, before every application and the poultice should not be left on till dry, nor too often repeated, which might cause an enlargement of the wounds. The diet should be light, the animal should be allowed very little exercise, and the general state of his health should be attended to. In dry parched weather, leathern boots are a great protection to the feet, when there is any tendency to soreness. The dog must be habituated to them, before he is taken out, or he will find them too great an annoyance, to permit him to attend to his duties. Should the toe nails grow inconveniently long, they had better be filed off, as they are apt to injure the feet, and prove an annoyance to the animal.

REMARKS ON ILLUSTRATIONS.

In presenting to the public what I believe to be faithful representations of sundry varieties of the Canine Species, I cannot dare presume, that even the *knowing ones* will pronounce them *all* to reflect the image of unadulterated stock; first, because there *does* exist a great variety of appearance, even in animals of pure and unsuspected blood; secondly, our ideas of purity seldom exactly agree, owing to a peculiarity of stamp, preferred by different fancy-breeders. Nevertheless, the animals have been selected by the Artist and myself. as the fairest specimens, which our united judgments could dictate, as the most likely to convey the idea of distinct Pedigree, to the total exclusion of Mongrelism. I can simply vouch for their being *true to the life*, and trust that in charity, all de fects may be antributed to the Dogs, rather than to the Artist or myself.

BRUNO.—The illustration represents a well trained animal, in possession of the Author. The breed owes its origin to the St. Bernard, Newfoundland and Alpine Shepherd-dog, although I commonly term them the St. Bernard Newfoundland. The Sire, old Bruno, was purchased of me by B. M. Whitlock, Esq., of New York city, by whom he is highly esteemed and treated like an educated dog should be. This breed is everything that can be desired, being equal in size, and (I think) superior to all others, in beauty, intelligence, activity and vigilance. Height from 30 to 34 inches; weight from 130 to 200 lbs.

ST. BERNARD.—These dogs take their name from a mountain of the Alps, celebrated for a Convent inhabited by Monks, who breed and train them for the purpose of carrying provisions to travellers, who may chance to lose their way in the deep and ofttimes impassable snows. They are from 29 to 34 inches in height; length from 6 1-2 to 7 feet, and when in good condition will weigh as high as 200 lbs. Their color is generally buff or light red, the muzzle dark

They are not presumed to be an original breed but appear rather to be a mixture of Spanish Mastiff and Bloodhound.

THE NEWFOUNDLAND is perhaps better known than the majority of breeds, being a general favorite. There are various stamps of Newfoundlands, varying both in shape, growth and hair, according to the latitude of their nativity. The pure should be entirely black. They may be greatly improved by a judicious cross, after which the colors of course are inclined to vary. On the Sea coast, he will subsist entirely on raw fish, and spends the greater part of his time in the water.

ST. BERNARD NEWFOUNDLAND, is a cross between the St. Bernard and Newfoundland. He is a fine large, handsome, majestic and respectable looking dog, remarkable in beauty, sagacity and intelligence. His height is from 30 to 34 inches, and I have had them weigh over 200 lbs. He appears to inherit the virtues of both Sire and Dam, without any of their failings. Their colors vary from jet-black down to light fawn-color.

BLOODHOUND is the largest of the Hound species, but his appearance and courage indicate a tinge of Mastiff or Bull-dog. The pure old fashion breed is nearly extinct, and various stamps of Dogs are now termed Bloodhounds. He is not naturally such a ferocious animal as his name might imply, but as he is trained to follow the scent of human blood, he is deservedly dreaded by those, who are unacquainted with him. He is principally renowned for catching Negroes, and when put on the scent of a man will follow it as true as the Harrier does the Hare.

Scotch Deer-hound appears to have originated in an amalgamation of Scotch Terrier and Greyhound. He is powerful, fleet and courageous, and measures sometimes over 30 inches in height. His hair is rough, and generally of a yellowish color. In him are combined the nerve of the Foxhound, with the fleetness of the Greyhound. These dogs are rare, and fetch occasionally enormous prices, as few ever own them but the Nobility and Gentry, who hold almost exclusive possession of the pure Stock.

Stag hound, Chanticleer.—A true English Staghound of the staunch old breed ; now all but extinct. This race of hounds is very rare, even in England ; the fast going modern Foxhound, (bred chiefly for speed) having banished the old breed from the kennels. In the days when this Hound was used, the hunter was a strong compact horse, not fast, but a good fencer, agreeing in every respect with the sturdy, deep-mouthed pack, he was called upon to follow. At present, the fashion is altered, and higher bred animals are required to keep pace with the pack before him.

FOXHOUND, JOLLYBOY.—This extraordinary Hound was bred in Patterson, N. J., and comes from a race of black and tan Foxhounds alike celebrated for their speed and mettle. His real time is not known, but from his astonishing performances, it is fair to presume he may outlast anything, than can be brought into competition with him. A glance at his short round barrel, his monstrous shoulder, the broad and ample quarters, the fire of his eye, and the resolute dare-devil expression of his face will be a sufficient guide, as to what the *tout ensemble* of a good lasting Foxhound should be made of. His owner challenges him, without hesitation, against any Hound, which England or the United States can produce, to run drag, Fox or Deer. No fence has been found too high for

THE MONGRELS.

MONGREL.

Call him Newfoundland, Turnspit, Pointer,
Skye!
Crooked leg, long back, snub nose and bleary
eye:
With Setter head, Hound-ear and Terrier-tail!
Whilst Pug and Poodle on the whole prevail!
A public nuisance, and the neighbor's pest;
His home the gutter, and the street his rest;
Nor road, nor path, nor byeway, but reveals
Some sneaking Yipyap, skulking at one's heels.
Incessant yelps, cries thief by night and day,
But thief in sight, the Mongrel shirks away;
Mocks the faint echo of each canine tone,
Yet flies impromptu, frightened at his own.
To title such a despicable brute,
Demands a sobriquet, his race to suit;
By dogdom doomed, of wit and merit stript,
Outcast, pleb-ian, Mongrel, nondescript,
But may exclaim some educated Cur:
"Why blast our race, by such contemptuous
slur?
Pause, pity, ponder thy polluted page,
Rude, raving rhymist, rest thy ranting rage;
Among us rare, the Mountebank or Scholar,
And rarer yet the Cur, that's worth a Dollar;
Yet treat us well, and train us like a Setter,
A Mongrel's word for't, we'd be ten times better."

him, no run too long, and no Hound sufficiently swift to show him the road.

HARRIER, "BARMAID."—An honest representation of an honest hunter. Small, light made and possessing wonderful power of nose, she is able to keep her place in the field, with the best of Foxhounds; often performing miracles in cold weather, when the leading hounds are at fault. Barmaid was never known to overrun her game. Our illustration gives her action, when running at full cry, and will be recognized by many, who have witnessed her performances.

BEAGLE is the smallest of the Hound Species. They were formerly hunted in packs, but since the introduction of faster stock, their use has been discontinued. He has superior scent and great endurance, and is the best dog in existence for rabbit-hunting, on account of his slow pace and diminutive size.

GREYHOUND (English) is perhaps the most elegant of all the hunting-breeds. His speed is supposed to equal that of the fastest race-horse. If thorough bred, he runs wholly by sight, which is superior to that of any other dog. In a coursing match, should he attempt to make use of his scenting powers, he would be ruled off the course, as foul-bred. They require great care and attention in hot climates, as on account of the thinness of their pelts, they are very susceptible of atmospheric changes.

GREYHOUND, Italian, is very similar to the English, but much smaller and too flimsy and delicate, to be of any service in the field, though certainly the most graceful of parlor-pets. Some, when full grown will not exceed 6 or 8 lbs. in weight.

POINTER is much similar to the Setter, in his natural instincts, and equally varies in size and color. He is more suitable than the latter for Sporting in hot weather, on account of his thinner covering. Several countries boast of their celebrated breeds of Pointers. My own opinion is that they are equally good in all latitudes, when they are well trained.

SETTER when well bred is a very elegant dog, and deservedly esteemed for his game-hunting propensities. His color, size and appearance vary (like the Pointer) according to the taste and judgment of the breeder, but as three or four shades often appear in the same litter, the idea of color regulating the quality of the an imal, can scarcely be supported. The Setter appears to originate from the Pointer and Spaniel. For hard work and endurance, he may be considered superior to the Pointer.

WATER SPANIEL is larger than the Cocker Spaniel, his ears are longer and his coat more curly. He is superior to all others for aquatic purposes, and is more particularly serviceable in duck-shooting. His disposition is of the most amiable, and his affection unwavering.

COCKER SPANIEL is very much used in England, in Woodcock and Snipe-shooting; is good on all kinds of game, rather inclined to be wild, is more difficult to train than Pointer or Setter. He is little used in the United States, as the method of training him is not generally understood. There is a great variety of *so called* Cocker Spaniels, varying in weight from 12 to 20 lbs. Their color is generally liver or liver and white. They appear never to tire, where either hair or feather is at stake.

KING CHARLES' SPANIEL.—This breed takes it name from Charles 2nd, who was the first to introduce them into England. Some suppose them to have originated in Japan, as there exists there a breed. somewhat similar yet larger. To be perfect, a Charles' Spaniel should have 7 good points: round head, short nose, long curly ears, large full eyes, color black and tan, without white, perfect symmetry of form, and under 10 lbs. weight. Such is the original of the illustration: cost 44 Guineas in London. He is now in my possession. A short time ago, one was sold at public auction in England, and realized the sum of 525 guineas or over 2600 Dollars! They would be good hunting dogs, were they not too much enfeebled by confinement, indulgence, &c.

BLENHEIM SPANIEL takes his name from a village near Oxford, England, where the breed has been kept particularly select. He is very much similiar in appearance to the King Charles, but generally more delicate and slender; they are both no doubt of the same origin. The Blenheim varies in color; orange and white, black and tan and white, &c., according to the fashion of the day.

ARCTIC-DOG.--The dog represented is of the smaller breed of Polar-dogs, and was brought to New York in one of the ships of the "*Kane Expedition.*" Weight about twenty pounds.

He is remarkable for his activity and vigilence, and his sense of hearing is far more acute than that of any other dog I have ever owned. He has pluck enough to face anything, but will never quarrel, except when jealous of attention, bestowed on others, when he becomes wholly ungovernable.

JAPAN DOG.—This dog is the property of Captain McClooney, and was brought by him in the Japan Expedition under Commodore Perry. He resembles slightly the Charley and Blenheim stock, but lacks their beauty and symmetry of form.

ENGLISH MASTIFF has a serious, majestic air, is of a noble and courageous temperament, disdaining even to exchange civilities with an ordinary cur, or to take offense at trifling insults from his inferiors. He is rather slow in his movements, and perhaps not as vigilant as some of his cotemporaries ; yet the terror imposed by his stern and resolute aspect may atone for his lack of activity. His height may be from 28 to 30 inches, and he is well proportioned and muscular.

BULL-DOG is the most courageous and unflinching of the whole canine race. The pure breed is now rarely to be seen, and is well nigh extinct. The cross with the Terrier, (either Scotch or English), produces a superior animal, rivaling the Bull in pluck, and converting his dogged independence into a lively amalgamation of activity, beauty and usefulness. Whatever horrid ideas may be connected with the word Bull-dog, we are indebted to him for much of the energy, pluck and endurance imparted to other breeds, which otherwise might have faded out.

BULL-TERRIER is a cross from the Bull-dog and Terrier, and is one of the most useful guard-dogs now in use. In the woods he is an overmatch for the Badger, Fox, Skunk, Coon, &c. His courage is equal to that of the Bull-dog, and none can excel him in activity, vigilance or sagacity. No animal is more abused, or less deserving of it. The illustration represents my *celebrated* Dog, Tiger, to whom I am indebted for seventeen years of active service. Tiger knew about all that a dog can know, did all that any dog could perform and was faithful even to death. (See his Life and Adventures, published by the Author.)

SCOTCH-TERRIER is a name now generally

given to every small sized dog, with a rough woolly pelt. The breed has varied perhaps more than any other, on account of the tendency in cross breeds to produce *something like* the original, and there is no regular standard, by which to test their purity. He is the hardiest of all dogs, very courageous and particularly zealous in the destruction of all kinds of hairy vermin.

Skye Terrier is originally from the Isle of Skye to the north of Scotland. He is very rough, with long body and short legs, has rather a weazley shape, and is a first rate rat killer.

Wire Terrier is a cross between the Scotch and English Terrier, and is quite as good as either of them for destroying rats and other vermin. Gay, tough and venturesome, he rushes forward, in spite of brake, briar or cat's claw.

English Terrier (black and tan), is an elegant animal, when finely bred and well cared for. The illustration represents a female of the true old fashion breed. These dogs are very quick and intelligent; generally excellent ratters and may be trained to hunt anything. They vary greatly in weight, from two to twenty-five pounds, having of late years been greatly refined by crossing with the Italian Greyhound. If persisted in, this produces some very elegant specimens, but their proportions generally lack symmetry, and they become delicate and unfit for active service.

POODLE is well known the world over, and is famous for his fantastic performances and gymnastic exercises. They vary exceedingly in size and appearance, &c., from the different effects of climate and usage. Weight varying from 2 to 60 lbs. They are without courage, and their instrinsic value has yet to be revealed.

COACH-DOG, when full bred is a very beautiful animal. If perfect, he should be evenly spotted from tip to tip. Each spot should be perfectly distinct and not interfere with another. There are several ramifications of these dogs, said to be natives of Denmark, Dalmatia, &c. They appear to form a stronger attachment to the horse, than any other animal, and are capable of performing long journeys, keeping exact pace with their favorite. The true breed is valuable and difficult to procure.

PRINCE-DOG, OR SIBERIAN BLOOD-HOUND.—Prince is the largest Dog known in modern times; measuring 36 1-2 inches in height, 7 feet, 9 inches in length, weighing over 200lbs.

This breed was probably well known to the Romans in days of yore, when the combat with wild beasts was a striking feature in the imperial pastimes. The Author had the honor of introducing this celebrated Dog to Her Majesty and the Court at Windsor Castle, when Prince was unanimously decided to be the King of Dogs. I am still in possession of the stock.

SHEPHERD DOG, Scotch Colly, may be termed the most faithful of all Dogs. He lives a life of solitude, consequently neither his manners nor his morals are corrupted. He is both master and slave to his flock, a perfect pattern of patience, fidelity and generalship.

There are sundry varieties of the Shepherd Dog, differing in size and feature; every canine belonging to a Shepherd, being dubbed with that title. The Scotch Colly weighs from 45 to 60 lbs.

THE TURNSPIT derives his name from his

avocation. Weight from 15 to 20 lbs. ; long low and bandy legged, resembling the German Beagle, though his nose is longer, and his ears shorter. He is snappish, sullen, and unsociable, and has little but a good set of teeth to recommend him.

THE PUG-DOG was once a very fashionable and appropriate appendage to an old maid. He is not unlike the Bull-dog, in appearance ; yet his very antipodes in merit : barks at everything, but turns his back upon the meanest foe. Color yellow, with black nose ; tail thoroughly curled ; weight from 15 to 25 lbs. His race is well nigh extinct, and who shall dare regret it ?

CHINESE HAIRLESS DOG.—A noted dish in the Celestial Empire. There is a variety of these Dogs. differing much in size, from 7 to 40 lbs. weight. In shape they are similar to the English Terrier. They are not very agreeable to the touch, and are adapted only for warm climates. They are active, intelligent and faithful, and worthy of a nobler fate than to be petted for the stew-pan, or pampered for the pot.

SLED-DOG.—These animals perform the duties of both Horse and Hound. Their endurance in harness is truly astonishing. They are accustomed to hard work, scanty fare and ill-usage: yet they never desert their post, or forsake their master. They are natives of the extreme northern latitudes, consequently ill-adapted to Southern climates.

To them we are partially indebted for the discoveries of Parry, Ross, M'Clintock, Kane &c.

PRACTICAL HINTS TO OWNERS OF PET DOGS, &c.

Give your dog a little less than he can eat, and a little more than he can drink. All food is better cooked. Avoid raw meat in hot weather. Keep your pet from the fire; give a comfortable bed, but don't cover up. Don't let him get too fat; if he become too corpulent, shorten his fare and increase his exercise; if need be, administer gentle aperients. Be careful in washing to rub dry, and wrap well up, till the trembling is past. Give your dog a careful examination at least once a week. Beware of fleas: they create great excitement and irritation, Mange, &c., producing fits and perhaps consumption and death. Avoid all salt meats; yet a little salt should be added to all that is in process of cooking. One good meal a day is enough for a sturdy dog; puppies and delicate animals had better be fed twice. To ensure a good watch dog, feed once a day, in the morning. His nocturnal vigils

will be inspirited by his abdominal yearnings. Feed at regular hours and give a little exercise *immediately* after, to avoid a domestic catastrophe. Be particularly careful in feeding puppies; they will always eat more than they can conveniently digest. Feed as little meat to them as possible, unless well amalgamated with cooked meal or vegetables. This rule is more or less applicable to the whole canine fraternity. Don't believe such indigestible nonsense, about a worm in a dog's tail, or under his tongue; place no faith in having his tail bitten off; don't waste the lump of insoluble brimstone in his water. Don't upbraid your dog for his indifference, if you allow him half-a-dozen masters. Don't administer more punishment to him than is absolutely necessary, and never forget to make it up with him after a scourging. Never let a *faux pas* pass unrebuked, nor a transgression unpardoned. Let puppies have plenty of exercise, and see that your watch dog has a staple, chain, collar and spring, that are perfectly reliable. Be careful to give cool shade in summer, and warm shelter in winter.

APPENDIX.

Mr. Edward Jesse, keeper of the Queens Park, London, in his "Anecdotes of Dogs," has shown great research and study on this noble animal, which has been truly styled "the most faithful friend of man." In the following pages will be found many good things from his work:

A French writer has boldly affirmed, that with the exception of women there is nothing so agreeable, or so necessary to the comfort of man, as the dog. This assertion may readily be disputed, but still it will be allowed that man, deprived of the companionship and services of the dog, would be a solitary and, in many respects, a helpless being. Let us look at the shepherd, as the evening closes in and his flock is dispersed over the almost inaccessible heights of mountains; they are speedily collected by his indefatigable dog—nor do his services end here: he guards either the flock or his masters' cottage by night, and a slight caress, and the coarsest food, satisfy him for all his trouble. The dog performs the services of a horse in the more northern regions. In the destruction of wild beasts, or the less dangerous stag, or in attacking the bull, the dog has proved himself to possess pre-eminent courage. In many instances he has died in the defence of his master. He has saved him from drowning, warned him of approaching danger, served him faithfully in poverty and distress, and if deprived of sight has gently led him about. When spoken to, he tries to hold a conversation by the movement of his tail or the expression of his eyes. If his master wants amusement in the field or wood, he is delighted to have an opportunity of procuring it for him; if he finds himself in solitude, his dog will be a cheerful and agreeable companion, and may be, when death comes, the last to forsake the grave of his beloved master.

There are a thousand little facts connected with dogs, which many, who do not love them as much as we do, may not have observed, but which all tend to devolop their character. For instance, every one knows the fondness of dogs for warmth, and that they never appear more contented than when reposing on the rug before a good fire. If, however, we quit the room, our dog leaves his warm berth, and places himself at the door, where he can the better hear our footsteps, and be ready to greet us when we re-enter. If we are preparing to take a walk, our dog is instantly aware of our intention. He frisks and jumps about, and is all eagerness to accompany us. If we are thoughtful or melancholy, he appears to sympathise with us; and, on the contrary, when we are disposed to be merry, he shows by his manner that he rejoices with us. We have often watched the effect which a change in our countenance would produce. If we frown or look severe, but without saying a word or uttering a sound, the effect is instantly seen by the ears dropping, and the eyes showing unhappiness. Before a dog, however, arrives at this knowledge of the human countenance, he must be the companion of your walks, repose at your feet, and receive his food from your hands: treated in this manner, the attachment of the dog is unbounded; be becomes fond, intelligent, and grateful. Whenever Stanislas, the unfortunate King of Poland, wrote to his daughter, he always concluded his letter with these words—"Tristan, my companion in misfortune, licks your feet:" thus showing that be bad still one friend who stuck to him in his adversity. Such is the animal whose propensities, instincts, and habits, we propose to illustrate by various anecdotes.

The propensities of the dog, and some of them are most extraordinary, appear to be independent of that instinct which Paley calls, "a propensity previous to experience, and independent of instruction." Some of these are hereditary, or derived from the habits of the parents, and are suited to the purposes to which each breed has long been and is still applied. In fact, their organs have a fitness or unfitness for certain functions without education;—for instance, a very young puppy of the St. Bernard breed of dogs, when taken on snow for the first time, will begin to scratch it with considerable eagerness. We have seen a young pointer of three or four weeks old stand steadily on first seeing poultry, and a well-bred terrier puppy will show a great deal of ferocity at the sight of a rat or mouse.

Some naturalists have endeavored to trace the origin of the dog from the fox; while others, and some of the most eminent ones, are of opinion that it sprung from the wolf. The former theory is out of the question. The wolf, perhaps, has some claim to be considered as the parent animal, and that he is susceptible of as strong attachment as the dog is proved by the following anecdote, related by Cuvier:

He informs us, that a young wolf was brought up as a dog, became familiar with every person whom he was in the habit of seeing, and in particular, followed his master everywhere, evincing evident chagrin at his absence, obeying his voice, and showing a degree of submission scarcely differing in any respect from that of the domesticated dog. His master, being obliged to be absent for a time, presented his pet to the Ménagerie du Roi, where the animal, confined in a den, continued disconsolate, and would scarcely eat his food. At length, however, his health returned, he became attached to his keepers, and appeared to have forgotten all his former affection; when, after an absence of eighteen months, his master returned. At the first word he uttered, the wolf, who had perceived him amongst the crowd, recognized him, and exhibited the most lively joy. On being set at liberty, the most affectionate caresses were lavished on his old master, such as the most attached dog would have shown after an absence of a few days.

A second separation was followed by similar

demonstrations of sorrow, which, however, again yielded to time. Three years passed, and the wolf was living happily in company with a dog, which had been placed with him, when his master again returned, and again the long-lost but still-remembered voice was instantly replied to by the most impatient cries, which were redoubled as soon as the poor animal was set at liberty; when rushing to his master, he threw his fore-feet on his shoulders, licking his face with the most lively joy, and menacing his keepers, who offered to remove him, and towards whom, not a moment before, he had been showing every mark of fondness.

A third separation, however, seemed to be too much for this faithful animal's temper. He became gloomy, desponding, refused his food, and for a long time his life appeared in great danger. His health at last returned, but he no longer suffered the caresses of any but his keeper, and towards strangers manifested the original savageness of his species.

It must, in fact, be always an interesting matter of inquiry respecting the descent of an animal so faithful to man, and so exclusively his associate and his friend, as the dog. Accordingly, this question has been entertained ever since Natural History took the rank of a science. But the origin of the dog is lost in antiquity. We find him occupying a place in the earliest pagan worship; his name has been given to one of the first-mentioned stars of the heavens, and his effigy may be seen in some of the most ancient works of art. Pliny was of opinion that there was no domestic animal without its unsubdued counterpart, and dogs are known to exist absolutely wild in various parts of the old and new world. The Dingo of New Holland, a magnificent animal of this kind, has been shown to be susceptible of mutual attachment in a singular degree, though none of the experiments yet made have proved that he is capable, like the domestic dog, of a similar attachment to man. The parentage of the wild dogs has been assigned to the tame species, strayed from the dominion of their masters. This, however, still remains a question, and there is reason to believe that the wild dog is just as much a native of the wilderness as the lion or tiger. If there be these doubts about an animal left for centuries in a state of nature, how can we expect to unravel the difficulties accumulated by ages of domestication? Who knows for a certainty the true prototype of the goat, the sheep, or ox?

To the unscientific reader such questions might appear idle, as having been settled from time immemorial; yet they have never been finally disposed of. The difficulty, as with the dog, may be connected with modifications of form and color, resulting from the long continued interference of man with the breed and habits of animals subjected to this sway.

Buffon was very eloquent in behalf of the claim of the sheep-dog to be considered as the true ancestor of all other varieties. Mr. Hunter would award this distinction to the wolf; supposing also that the jackal is the same animal a step further advanced towards civilization, or perhaps the dog returned to its wild state. As the affinity between wolf, jackal, fox, and dog, cannot fail to attract the notice of the most superficial observer; so he may ask if they do not all really belong to one species, modified by varieties of climate, food, and education? If answered in the negative, he would want to know what constitutes a species, little thinking that this question, apparently so simple, involves one of the nicest problems in natural history. Difference of form will scarcely avail us here, for the pug, greyhound, and spaniel, are wider apart in this respect, than many dogs and the wild animals just named. It has often been said that these varieties in the dog have arisen from artificial habits and breeding through a long succession of years. This seems very like mere conjecture. Can the greyhound be trained to the pointer's scent or the spaniel to the bulldog's ferocity? But admitting the causes assigned to be adequate to the effects, then the forms would be temporary, and those of a permanent kind only would serve our purpose. Of this nature is the shape of the pupil of the eye, which may be noticed somewhat particularly, not merely to make it plain to those who have never thought on the subject, but with the hope of leading them to reflections on this wondrous inlet to half our knowledge, the more especially as the part in question may be examined by any one in his own person by the help of a looking-glass. In the front of the eye then, just behind the transparent surface, there is a sort of curtain called the *iris*, about the middle of which is a round hole. This is the pupil, and you will observe that it contracts in a strong light, and dilates in a weaker one, the object of which is to regulate the quantity of light admitted into the eye. Now the figure of the pupil is not the same in all animals. In the horse it is oval; in the wolf, jackal, and dog, it is round, like our own, however contracted; but in the fox, as in the cat, the pupil contracts vertically into an elongated figure, like the section of a lens, and even to a sort of slit, if the light be very strong.

This is a permanent character, not affected, as far as is at present known, by any artificial or natural circumstances to which the dog has been subjected. Naturalists, therefore, have seized upon this character as the ground for a division of animals of the dog kind, the great genus *Canis* of Linnæus, into two groups, the diurnal and nocturnal; not to imply that these habits necessarily belong to all the individuals composing either of these divisions, for that would be untrue, but simply that the figure of the pupils corresponds with that frequently distinguishing day-roaming animals from those that prowl only by night.

We will give a few anecdotes to show how different this animal is in his specific character to the wolf, and that he has a natural tendency to acknowledge man as his friend and protector, an instinct never shown by the wolf.

In Ceylon there are a great number of what are called wild dogs, that is, dogs who have no master, and who haunt villages and jungles, picking up what food they are able to find. If you meet one of these neglected animals, and only look at him with an expression of kindness, from that moment he attaches himself to you, owns you for his master, and will remain faithful to you for the remainder of his life.

"Man," says Burns, "is the God of the dog; he knows no other; and see how he worships him! With what reverence he crouches at his feet, with what reverence he looks up to him, with what delight he fawns upon him, and with what cheerful alacrity he obeys him!"

Such is the animal which the brutality of man subjects to so much ill-treatment; its character depends very much on that of his master, kindness and confidence produce the same qualities in the dog, while ill-usage makes him sullen and distrustful of beings far more brutal than himself.

We have had many opportunities of observing how readily dogs comprehend language, and how they are aware when they are the subject of conversation. A gentleman once said in the hearing of an old and favorite dog, who was at the time basking in the sun,—"must have Ponto killed, for he gets old and is offensive."

The dog slunk away, and never came near his master afterwards. Many similar anecdotes might be brought forward, but I will mention one which Captain Brown tells us he received himself from Sir Walter Scott.

"The wisest dog I ever had," said Sir Walter, "was what is called the bulldog terrier. I taught him to understand a great many words, insomuch that I am positive that the communication betwixt the canine species and ourselves might be greatly enlarged. Camp once bit the baker, who was bringing bread to the family. I beat him, and explained the enormity of his offence; after which, to the last of his life, he never heard the least allusion to the story, in what ever voice or tone it was mentioned, without getting up and retiring into the darkest corner of the room, with great appearance of distress. Then if you said, "the baker was well paid," or, "the baker was not hurt after all," Camp came forth from his hiding-place, capered, and barked, and rejoiced. When he was unable, towards the end of his life, to attend me when on horseback, he used to watch for my return, and the servant would tell him "his master was coming down the hill, or through the moor," and although he did not use any gesture to explain his meaning, Camp was never known to mistake him, but either went out at the front to go up the hill, or at the back to get down to the moor-side. He certainly had a singular knowledge of spoken language." An anecdote from Sir Walter Scott must be always pleasing.

Mr. Smellie, in his "Philosophy of Natural History," mentions a curious instance of the intellectual faculty of a dog. He states that "a grocer in Edinburgh had one which for some time amused and astonished the people in the neighbourhood. A man who went through the streets ringing a bell and selling pies, happened one day to treat this dog with a pie. The next time he heard the pieman's bell he ran impetuously toward him, seized him by the coat and would not suffer him to pass. The pieman, who understood what the animal wanted, showed him a penny, and pointed to his master, who stood at the street-door, and saw what was going on. The dog immediately supplicated his master by many humble gestures and looks, and on receiving a penny he instantly carried it in his mouth to the pieman, and received his pie. This traffic between the pieman and the grocer's dog continued to be daily practiced for several months."

The affections which some dogs show to their masters and mistresses is not only very often surprising, but even affecting. An instance of this lately occured at Brighton. The wife of a member of the town council at that place had been an invalid for some time, and at last was confined to her bed. During this period she was constantly attended by a faithful and affectionate dog, who either slept in her room or outside her door. She died, was buried, and the dog followed the remains of his beloved mistress to her grave. After the funeral, the husband and his friends returned to the house, and while they were partaking of some refreshment the dog put his paws on his master's arm, as if to attract his attention, looked wistfully in his face, and then laid down and instantly expired.

In giving miscellaneous anecdotes in order to show the general character of the dog, we will mention the following very curious one:

During a very severe frost and fall of snow in Scotland, the fowls did not make their appearance at the hour when they usually retired to roost, and no one knew what had become of them; the house-dog at last entered the kitchen, having in his mouth a hen, apparently dead. Forcing his way to the fire, the sagacious animal laid his charge down upon the warm hearth, and immediately set off. He soon came again with another, which he deposited in the same place, and so continued till the whole of the poor birds were rescued. Wandering about the stack-yard, the fowls had become quite benumbed by the extreme cold, and had crowded together, when the dog observing them, effected their deliverance, for they all revived by the warmth of the fire.

Mr. Bell, in his "History of British Quadrupeds," gives us the following fact of a dog belonging to a friend of his. This gentleman dropped a louis d'or one morning, when he was on the point of leaving his house. On returning late at night, he was told by his servant that the dog had fallen sick, and refused to eat, and, what appeared very strange, she would not suffer him to take her food away from before her, but had been lying with her nose close to the vessel, without attempting to touch it. On Mr. Bell's friend entering the room, the dog instantly jumped upon him, laid the money at his feet, and began to devour his victuals with great voracity.

"It is a curious fact, says Mr. Jesse, that dogs can count time. I had, when a boy, a favorite terrier, which always went with me to church. My mother thinking that he attracted too much attention, ordered the servant to fasten him up every Sunday morning. He did so once or twice, but never afterwards. Trim concealed himself every Sunday morning, and either met me as I entered the church, or I found him under my seat in the pew." Mr. Southey, in his "Omniana," informs us that he knew of a dog, which was brought up by a Catholic and afterwards sold to a Protestant, but still refused to eat any meat on a Friday.

A gentleman who had a dog of a most endearing disposition, was obliged to go on a journey periodically once a-month. His stay was short, and his departure and return very regular, and without variation. The dog always grew uneasy when he first lost his master, and moped in a corner, but recovered himself gradually as the time for his return approached; which he knew to an hour, nay to a minute. When he was convinced that his master was on the road, at no great distance from home, he flew all over the house; and if the street door happened to be shut, he would suffer no servant to have any rest until it was opened. The moment he obtained his freedom away he went, and to a certainty met his benefactor about two miles from town. He played and frolicked about him till he had obtained one of his gloves, with which he ran or rather flew home, entered the house, laid it down in the middle of the room, and danced around it. When he had sufficiently amused himself in this manner, out of the house he flew, returned to meet his master, and ran before him, or gambolled by his side, till he arrived with him at home. "I know not (says Mr. Dibdin, who relates this anecdote), how frequently this was repeated; but it lasted till the old gentleman was infirm, and incapable of continuing his journeys.

Colonel Hamilton Smith, in the "Cyclopædia of Natural History," mentions a curious instance of fidelity and sagacity in a dog. He informs us that "in the neigborhood of Cupar, in the county of Fife, there lived two dogs, mortal enemies to each other, and who always fought desperately whenever they met. Capt. R—— was the master of one of them, and the other belonged to a neighboring farmer. Capt. R——'s dog was in the practice of going messages, and even of bringing butchers' meat and other articles from Cupar. One day, while returning charged with a basket containing some pieces of mutton, he was attaked by some of the curs of the town, who, no doubt, thought the prize worth contending for. The assault was fierce, and of some duration; but the messenger, after doing his utmost, was overpowered and compelled to yield up the basket, though not before he had secured a part of its contents. The piece saved from the wreck he ran off with, at full speed, to the quarters of his old enemy, at whose feet he laid it down, stretching himself beside it till he had eaten it up. A few snuffs, a few whispers in the ear, and other dog-like courtesies, were then exchanged; after which they both set off together for Cupar, where they worried almost every dog in the town; and, what is more remarkable, they never afterwards quarreled, but were always on friendly terms."

That society and culture soften and moderate the passion of dogs cannot be doubted, and they constantly imbibe feelings from those of their master. Thus, if he is a coward, his dog is generally found to be one. Dogs are, however, in many respects, rational beings; and some proofs of this will be given in the present work. They will watch the countenance of their master—they will understand words which, though addressed to others, they will apply to themselves, and act accordingly. Thus a dog, which from its mangy state, was ordered to be destroyed, took the first opportunity of quitting the ship, and would never afterwards come near a sailor belonging to it. If I desire the servant to wash a little terrier, who is apparently asleep at my feet, he will quit the room, and hide himself for some hours. A dog, though pressed with hunger, will never seize a piece of meat in presence of his master, though with his eyes, his movements, and his voice, he will make the most humble and expressive petition. Is not this reasoning?

Both the wild and domestic dog, appear to be possessed of and to exercise forethought. They will bury or hide food, which they are unable to consume at once, and return for it. But the domestic dog, perhaps gives stronger proofs of forethought; and we will give an instance of it. A large metal pot, turned on one side, in which a great quantity of porridge had been boiled, was set before a Newfoundland puppy of three or four months old. At first, he contented himself by licking off portions of the oatmeal which adhered to the interior, but finding this unsatisfactory, he scraped the morsels with his fore-paws into a heap, and then ate the whole at once. We had a dog, who, having scalded his tongue, always afterwards, when given his milk and water at breakfast, put his paw very cautiously into the saucer, to see if the liquid was too hot, before he would touch it with his tongue.

Dogs have frequently been known to hunt in couples; that is, to assist each other in securing their prey:

At Palermo, in Sicily, there is an extraordinary quantity of dogs wandering about without owners. Amongst the number, two more particularly distinguished themselves for their animosity to cats. One day they were in pursuit of a cat, which, seeing no other place of refuge near, made her escape into a long earthen water-pipe which was lying on the ground. These two inseparable companions, who always supported each other, pursued the cat to the pipe, where they were seen to stop, and apparently to consult each other as to what was to be done to deceive and get possession of the poor cat. After they had stood a short time they divided, taking post at each each end of the pipe, and began to bark alternately, changing places while so doing, thus giving the cat reason to suppose that they were both at one end, in order to induce her to come out. This manœuver had a successful result, and the cheated cat left her hiding-place. Scarcely had she ventured out, when she was seized by one of the dogs; the other hastened to his assistance, and in a few moments deprived her of life.

In the small town of Melbourne, in Derbyshire, cocks and hens may be seen running about the streets. One day a game cock attacked a small bantam, and they fought furiously, the bantam having of course the worst of it. Some persons were standing about looking at the fight, when my informant's house-dog suddenly darted out, snatched up the bantam in his mouth, and carried it into his house. Several of the spectators followed, believing that the poor fowl would be killed and eaten by the dog; but his intentions were of a more benevolent nature. After guarding the entrance of the kennel for some time, he trotted down the yard into the street, looking about to the right and left, and seeing that the coast was clear, he went back again, and once more returned with his *protégé* in his mouth, safely deposited him in the street, and then walked quietly away. How few human beings would have acted as this dog had done!

Here is another curious anecdote from Mr. Davy's work. He says that the cook in the house of a friend of his, a lady on whose accuracy he could rely, and from whom he had the anecdote, missed a marrow-bone. Suspicion fell on a well-behaved dog—a great favorite, and up to the time distinguished for his honesty. He was charged with the theft; he hung down his tail, and for a day or two was altered in his manner, having become shy, sullen, and sheepish. In this mood he continued, till, to the amusement of the cook, he brought back the bone and laid it at her feet. Then, with the restoration of her property, he resumed his cheerful manner. How can we interpret this conduct of the dog better than by supposing that he was aware he had done amiss, and that the evil-doing preyed on him till he had made restitution? Was not this a kind of moral sense?

If a dog finds a bone while he is accompanying his master in a walk, he does not stay behind to gnaw it, but runs some distance in advance, attacks the bone, waits till his master comes up, and then proceeds forward again with it. By acting in this manner, he never loses sight of his master.

A dog has been known to convey food to another of his species who was tied up and pining for want of it. A dog has frequently been seen to plunge voluntarily into a rapid stream, to rescue another that was in danger of drowning. He has defended helpless curs from the attacks of other dogs, and learns to apportion punishment according to the provocation received, frequently disdaining to exercise his power and strength on a weaker adversary. Repeated provocation will, however, excite revenge. For instance, a Newfoundland dog was quietly eating his mess of broth and broken scraps. While so employed, a turkey endeavored to share the meal with him. The dog growled, and displayed his teeth. The intruder retired for a moment, but quickly returned to the charge, and was again "warned off," with a like result. After three or four attempts of the same kind, the dog became provoked, gave a sudden ferocious growl, bit off the delinquent's head, and then quietly finished his meal, without bestowing any further attention on his victim.

The celebrated Leibnitz related to the French Academy an account of a dog he had seen which was taught to speak, and could call in an intelligible manner for tea, coffee, chocolate, &c.

The dog was of a middling size, and the property of a peasant in Saxony. A little boy, the peasant's son, imagined that he perceived in the dog's voice an indistinct resemblance to certain words, and was, therefore, determined to teach him to speak distinctly. For this purpose he spared neither time nor pains with his pupil, who was about three years old when his learned education commenced; and at length he made such progress in language, as to be able to articulate no less than thirty words. It appears, however, that he was somewhat of a truant, and not very willingly exerted his talents, being rather pressed into the service of literature, and it was necessary that the words should be first pronounced to him each time before he spoke. The French Academicians who mention this anecdote, add, that unless they had received the testimony of so great a man as Leibnitz, they should scarcely have dared to relate the circumstance.

"An invalid gentleman" says Mr. Jesse, "who resided for some years on Ham Common, in Surrey, had a dog which distinctly pronounced John, William, and two or three other words.

A medical friend of mine who attended this gentleman has frequently heard the animal utter these words; and a female relative of his, who was often at a visit at his house, assures me of the fact. Indeed it need not be doubted."

A dog, belonging to the late Dr. Robert Hooper, had been in the constant habit of performing various little personal services for his master, such as fetching his slippers, &c. It happened one day that Dr. Hooper had been detained by his professional duties much beyond his usual dinner hour. The dog impatiently waited for his arrival, and he at last returned, weary and hungry. After showing his pleasure at the arrival of his master, greeting him with his usual attention, the animal remained tolerably quiet until he conceived a reasonable time had elapsed for the preparation of the Doctor's dinner. As it did not, however, make its appearance, the dog went into the kitchen, seized with his mouth a half-broiled beef-steak, with which he hastened back to his master, placing it on the table-cloth before him.

The following anecdote shows extraordinary sense, if not reasoning faculty, in the dog:—

A lady of high rank has a sort of colley, or Scotch shepherd-dog. When he is ordered to ring the bell, he does so; but if he is told to ring the bell when the servant is in the room whose duty it is to attend, he refuses, and then the following occurrence takes place. His mistress says, "Ring the bell, dog." The dog looks at the servant, and then barks his bow wow, once or twice. The order is repeated two or three times. At last the dog lays hold of the servant's coat in a significant manner, just as if he had said to him—"Don't you hear that I am to ring the bell for you?—come, my lady." His mistress always had her shoes warmed before she put them on, but one day during the hot weather her maid was putting them on without their having been previously placed before the fire. When the dog saw this he immediately interfered, expressing the greatest indignation at the maid's negligence. He took the shoes from her, carried them to the fire, and after they had been warmed as usual, he brought them back to his mistress with much apparent satisfaction, evidently intending to say, if he could, "It is all right now."

At Albany in Worcestershire, at the seat of Admiral Maling, a dog went every day to meet the mail, and brought the bag in his mouth to the house. The distance was about an eighth of a mile. The dog usually received a meal of meat as his reward. The servants having, on *one day only*, neglected to give him his accustomed meal, the dog on the arrival of the next mail buried the bag, nor was it found without considerable search.

A gentleman residing in Denmark, M. Decouick, one of the king's privy councillors, found that he had a remarkable dog. It was the habit of Mr. Decouick to leave Copenhagen on Fridays for Drovengourd, his country seat. If he did not arrive there on the Friday evening, the dog would invariably be found at Copenhagen on Saturday morning, in search of his master. Hydrophobia becoming common, all dogs were shot that were found running about, an exception being made in the case of Mr. Decouick's dog, on account of his sagacity and fidelity, a distinctive mark being placed upon him.

The following anecdotes are from Daniel's "Rural Sports:"—

Dr. Beattie, in one of his ingenious and elegant essays, relates a story, in his own knowledge, of a gentleman's life being saved, who fell beneath the ice, by his dog's going in quest of assistance, and almost forcibly dragging a farmer to the spot.

Mr. Vaillant describes the losing of a bitch while travelling in Africa, when after firing his gun, and fruitlessly searching for her, he despatched one of his attendants, to return by the way they had proceeded; when she was found at about two leagues' distance, seated by the side of a chair and basket, which had dropped unperceived from his wagon: an instance of attentive fidelity, which must have proved fatal to the animal, either from hunger or beasts of prey, had she not been luckily discovered.

As instances of the dog's sagacity, the following are submitted: In crossing the mountain St. Gothard, near Airola, the Chevalier Gaspard de Brandenberg and his servant were buried by an avalanche; his dog, who escaped the heap of snow, did not quit the place where he had lost his master: this was, fortunately, not far from the convent; the animal howled, ran to the convent frequently, and then returned. Struck by his perseverance, the next morning the people from the house followed him; he led them directly to the spot, scratched the snow, and after thirty-six hours passed beneath it, the chevalier and his domestic were taken out safe, hearing distinctly during their confinement the howling of the dog and the discourse of their deliverers. Sensible that to the sagacity and fondness of this creature he owed his life, the gentleman ordered by his will that he should be represented on his tomb with his dog; and at Zug, in the church of St. Oswald, where he was buried in 1728, they still show the monument and the effigy of this gentleman, with the dog lying at his feet.

Colonel Hutchinson relates the following anecdote:—

"A cousin of one of my brother-officers was taking a walk at Tunbridge Wells, when a strange Newfoundland snatched her parasol from her hand, and carried it off. The lady followed the dog, who kept ahead, constantly looking back to see if she followed. The dog at length stopped at a confectioners, and went in, followed by the lady, who, as the dog would not resign it, applied to the shopman for assistance. He then told her that it was an old trick of the dog's to get a bun, and that if she would give him one he would return the property. She cheerfully did so, and the dog as willingly made the exchange."

The above anecdote proves that dogs are no

mean observers of countenances, and that he had satisfied himself by a previous scrutiny as to the probability of his delinquencies being forgiven.

We will give a laughable philosophical account of dogs, under the supposition of a transmigration of souls, and with their general natural history from Linæus and Buffon, from a facetious believer in the art of distinguishing at the sight of any creature, from what class of animals his soul is derived.

The souls of deceased bailiffs and common constables are in the bodies of setting dogs and pointers; the terriers are inhabited by trading justices; the bloodhounds were formerly a set of informers, thief-takers, and false evidences; the spaniels were heretofore courtiers, hangers-on of administrations, and hack journal-writers, all of whom preserve their primitive qualities of fawning on their feeders, licking their hands, and snarling and snapping at all who offer to offend their master; a former train of gamblers and black-legs are now embodied in that species of dog called lurchers; bull-dogs and mastiffs were once butchers and drovers; greyhounds and hounds owe their animation to country squires and foxhunters; little whiffling, useless lap-dogs, draw their existence from the quondam beau; macaronics, and gentlemen of the tippy, still being the playthings of ladies, and used for their diversion. There are also a set of sad dogs derived from attornies; and puppies, who were in past time attornies' clerks, shopmen to retail haberdashers, men-milliners, &c. &c. Turnspits are animated by old aldermen, who still enjoy the smell of the roast meat; that droning, snarling species, styled Dutch pugs, have been fellows of colleges: and that faithful, useful tribe of shepherd's dogs, were, in days of yore, members of parliament, who guarded the flock, and protected the sheep from wolves and thieves, although indeed of late some have turned sheep-biters, and worried those they ought to have defended.

The manner in which the shepherds of the Pyrenees employ their peculiar breed of dogs, which are large, long-haired, of a tawny white color, and a very strong build, with a ferocious temper, exhibits a vivid instance of the trust they repose in the courage and fidelity of these animals, and of the virtues by which they merit and reward it. Attended by three or more dogs, the shepherds will take their numerous flocks at early dawn to the part of the mountain side which is destined for their pasture. Having counted them, they descend to follow other occupations, and commit the guardianship of the sheep to the sole watchfulness of the dogs. It has been frequently known, that when wolves have approached, the three sentinels would walk round and round the flock, gradually compressing them into so small a circle that one dog might with ease overlook and protect them, and that this measure of caution being executed, the remaining two would set forth to engage the enemy, over whom, it is said, they invariably triumph.

It is now settled, as a philosophical question, that the instruction communicated to dogs, as well as various other animals, has an hereditary effect on the progeny. If a dog be taught to perform certain feats, the young of that dog will be much easier initiated in the same feats than other dogs. Thus, the existing races of English pointers are greatly more accomplished in their required duties than the original race of Spanish pointers. Dogs of the St. Bernard variety inherit the faculty of tracking footsteps in the snow. A gentleman of our acquaintance, and of scientific acquirements, obtained some years ago a pup, which had been produced in London by a female of the celebrated St. Bernard breed. The young animal was brought to Scotland, where it was never observed to give any particular tokens of a power of tracking footsteps until winter, when the ground became covered with snow. It *then* showed the most active inclination to follow footsteps; and so great was its power of doing so under these circumstances, that, when its master had crossed a field in the most curvilinear way, and caused other persons to cross his path in all directions, it nevertheless followed his course with the greatest precision. Here was a perfect revival of the habit of its Alpine fathers, with a degree of specialty as to external conditions at which, it seems to us, we cannot sufficiently wonder.

Such are some of the qualities of dogs in a state of domestication, and let us hope that the anecdotes related of them will tend to insure for them that love and gratitude to which their own fine disposition and noble character give them a claim from us.

It is pleasing to observe that men of the highest acquirements and most elevated minds have bestowed their sincere attachment upon their favorite canine companions; for kindness to animals is, perhaps, as strong an indication of the possession of generous sentiments as any that can be adduced. The late Lord Grenville, a distinguished statesman, an elegant scholar, and an amiable man, affords an illustration of the opinion: It is thus that he eloquently makes his favorite Zephyr speak:

"Captum oculis, senioque hebetem, morboque gravatum,
Dulcis here, antiquo me quod amore foves,
Suave habet et carum Zephyrus tuus, et leviore
Se sentit mortis conditione premi.
Interiêre quidem, tibi quæ placuisse solebant,
Et formæ dotes, et facile ingenium:
Deficiunt sensus, tremulæ scintillula vitæ
Vix micat, in cinerem mox abitura brevem.
Sola manet, veruli tibi nec despecta ministri,
Mens grata, ipsaque in morte memor domini.
Hanc tu igitur, pro blanditiis molique lepore,
Et promta ad nutus sedulitate tuos,
Pro saltu cursuque levi, lusuque protervo,
Hanc nostri extremum pignus amoris habe.
Jamque vale! Elysii subeo loca læta, piorum
Quæ dat Persephone manibus esse canum."

Pope says, that history is more full of examples of fidelity in the dog than in friends: and Lord Byron characterises him as—

"in life the firmest friend,
The first to welcome, foremost to defend;
Whose honest heart is still his master's own;
Whose labors, fights, lives, breathes for him alone;"

and truly indeed may be called

"The rich man's guardian, and the poor man's friend."

CANINE SUICIDE.

In Bethlehem, Pa., there lived, a few years ago, a man named P., who kept a saloon by the side of the railroad, and was the owner of a fine Newfoundland dog, of great sagacity. The saloon was often visited by boisterous and belligerent customers, who were "spoiling for a fight," and considered a bar-tender as presenting the best subject for a pummeling. In all such cases Mr. P. only had to say "Major," and the big Newfoundland had his paws on the shoulders of the pugnacious customer, looking him in the face. Two or three admonishing words from his capacious mouth was always a sufficient warning to keep the peace. He often amused the barroom crowd by his various tricks, among them was that of taking the hat from the head of any one in the room. Once a stranger came into the saloon to get some refreshments while waiting for the train. P. wished to show some half-dozen loungers Major's tricks, and ordered him to remove the stranger's hat. Major did as ordered, but the hair also came with the hat. The manœuver frightened the gentleman badly, and Mr. P., seeing the hair pealed from the gentleman's head, was more frightened than the stranger, and made haste to make amends. Major had great friendship for a little dog, a cross between the Poodle and the Scotch terrier. The little "Prince" was often set upon by his larger neighbors, and generally got the worst of it. In such cases he would sally forth in quest of his friend Major, when the fight was renewed and his assailant punished for his temerity. The little fellow was often, in summer time, partly sheared, which gave him, in the eyes of some, an ugly appearance. If any one made a derogatory remark about him, he noticed it, and showed his teeth in a very passionate manner. If Major was along, he also raised his voice in protest of any disapproval of his friend's looks. Major's master occasionally took too much of what he dispensed to others, and one evening, after sending Major to the field for the horses, which he drove up in good style, as was his practice, he followed his master up stairs. P., not finding wife or child to maltreat, kicked poor Major down stairs, injuring his spine. He dragged out a miserable existence for a few months; but becoming tired of life, he laid himself across the railroad track that fronted the door. He saw the locomotive coming, and when it neared him, he turned his head away, and allowed the train to crush him. This was witnessed by dozens of people, who knew it to be a deliberate case of suicide.

Another Newfoundland was installed in Major's place. The brutal master undertook to kick him around, but we are happy to say not without resentment, for he turned upon him, seized him by the throat, and would have choked him to death had not his cries brought the bar-keeper to his assistance.

The newspapers of the present week contain an account of a highly prized Newfoundland dog in Wakefield, Mass., after tugging at his muzzle, placed on him in accordance with the law, became despondent, and soon afterward jumped into the pond and drowned himself.

The owner of an old watch dog some where in the State of Wisconsin, seeing that the dog was useless, and rather troublesome in consequence of age, expressed his intention of shooting the old fellow. This was said in the hearing of the dog, and within an hour he was missing, and was found a few days afterwards in a pond near the house, where it was supposed that he had committed "dog-icide" by drowning himself.

A Canine Doctor.—There is a dog on

Staten Island, that seems to be a sort of physician among the canines in his neighborhood. If what we hear of this dog is true, he is a wonder indeed. It is said that whenever he meets with any other dog that is sick, he will by some mysterious intelligence induce the canine invalid, to follow him to the fields, and there eat of some grasses or weed, that in a few days effect a cure of the sick one. Several persons owners of dogs in the neighborhood, say from what they have witnessed that they believe, what is above stated.

Mr. H. McDonald, in his lecture on oddness gives the following anecdotes about dogs :—

I once heard of a dog, from his earliest puppyhood would walk twice around his food before touching it, and always to the left. If called away by his owner before he had gone fully around the second time, he would finish the circle from the point or place at which he had left off. On one occasion while his master kept him at a distance, his meat was taken up and laid on a bench. But on returning replaced it in nearly the exact spot it had been taken from, and then finished his ring movement. The diameter of the circles were as nearly uniform, as a man might have them without measurment.

and were about four and a half feet. I will not attempt to explain or say what was the cause of this oddity. But as the owner of the dog averred that he had not been taught,and instinct it could hardly be called, I set it down to a habit acquired by circumstances.

A most curious trick of a couple of dogs I remember to have heard often in my boyhood, and as the family in which the dogs were owned, were neighbors and friends of my Father's family. My memory was thoroughly impressed with the story, which is a true one. The two dogs named respectively Carlo and Ponto, were of the large mastiff breed, and besides being excellent watch dogs, were also safe companions or escorts to take along for protection against insult or attack of any kind. Now it so happened that one of the daughters of the family alluded too, who I shall call Miss Lena, was invited out to an afternoon quilting party, that in the evening was to be turned into a party for singing, and engaging in some of the old fashioned party plays, and of course the young men of their acquaintance were to be present after tea time. It further happened that among these young men there was one who was introduced to Miss Lena, and who during the evening solicited the honor of seeing her home, a request that was readily granted. At the proper hour perhaps 12 P. M. they started homeward a distance of over two miles, Lena's two four footed guardians, who had waited for her from the middle of the afternoon, joining in the escort. They did not however wag their tails, nor go bounding ahead nor stop to lick their Mistress' hand, as was their wont on other occasions, but simply trotted along behind the young couple in a sullen sort of a way with heads downward, and noses near together, as if in an undertone conversation. But when about a quarter of a mile on the way, Carlo without even a warning, gravely laid hold of Miss Lena's young man escort by the leg of his trousers, and would not permit him to move on any further, and neither the threats, blows, nor coaxings, of Miss Lena, could induce him to let go his hold. .The other dog took no part in the arrest, but trotted briskly a few yards ahead, indicating that he was ready for escort duty. The gentleman suggested to the young lady to accept the offer apparently made by Ponto, and that after she had started he would be set free, she did so reluctantly *of course*, and was soon joined by Carlo. The escort did not deem it healthy to make an effort to regain his position. Now the question that naturally presents itself is, were the dogs jealous of the attentions of the rival escort, and I think all will admit that such was the fact. If so how did they arrange their plan of revenge, on their rival? Is there a language by which animals can make known their thoughts to each other. It almost seems as if it was so. The story may seem like a very strange one, and though I am certain of its truth, it does nevertheless seem odd even to me.

Some years ago a large Newfoundland dog was honored with a medal, upon which was inscribed "A distinguished member of the Humane Society." Among the well-authenticated accounts of his usefulness is that of rescuing the crew of a vessel driven on the beach of Lydd, in Kent. Eight poor fellows were crying for help, but no boat could live in endeavoring to go to their assistance. At length a gentleman came on the beach accompanied by a Newfoundland dog. He directed the attention of the animal to the vessel, and put a short stick in his mouth. The intelligent and courageous fellow at once understood his meaning, springing into the sea, he fought his way through the waves. He could not, however, get close enough to the vessel to deliver that with which he was charged; but the crew understood what was meant, and they made fast a rope to another piece of wood, and threw it toward him. The noble creature dropped the one in his mouth, and seized that which had been cast to him, and then, with a degree of strength and determination scarcely credible—for he was again and again lost under the waves—he dragged it through the surge, and delivered it to his master; a line of communication was thus formed with the boat, and all on board were saved.

"JUNO" was a dog in which were mingled the blood of the spaniel and Newfoundland, and descended from a family remarkable for intelligence; for with dogs, even more than with men, talents are hereditary. This playful, intelligent creature, without any instruction, performed so many feats that she won a wide celebrity. So fond was she of her reasoning playmates, that she would at any time abandon her puppies to have a romp with the children. As a nurse, she took care of "the baby," and would follow it about, pick up its playthings, rock its cradle, and carefully restore to its hands the "chicken bone," for the moment dropped on the floor. Having once accompanied her master on a fishing excursion, she afterward would dig angleworms, draw the fishing-rod from its hooks, and insist in the stable that the horse should be saddled, and then lead the animal by the bridle up to the door. Her kind care extended to the chickens and ducks, and if any of the little ones were lamed or died, she at nightfall took them to their respective owners, and thrust them under the maternal wing. When the garden was made Juno seemed to admire the nicely-arranged beds, and throughout the whole summer, looked through the palings with indignation at what she supposed to be the intruding plants in the nicely-prepared ground.

Juno never would allow the servants to possess in peace any property once belonging to her master, mistress, or their children, which was not formally given away in her presence; in that case, she never noticed the articles at all. In New Orleans this dog attracted a great deal of attention, because she would not touch the poisoned sausages thrown into the street. She did not confine her useful labors exclusively to those who owned her, but would restore lost property, when she met with it, that belonged to any of the neighbors. She appeared to understand the meaning of words, and would instantly show by her manner how perfectly she comprehended the passing conversation. If any subject was alluded to in which she took an interest, she would bark and caper about, and designate as far as possible the different things alluded to. She would remain perfectly quiet, with an affectionate eye alone upon her master, through long discussions on politics or philosophy; but let anything be said about angling or hunting, about the poultry in the yard, or kindred subjects, and she would go almost crazy with delight. This dog, combining within herself the qualities of the two most intelligent breeds of her kind, seemed but little removed from a reasoning, intelligent being; there were, at times, expressions in her eye, of affection, of thought, of sorrow, of joy, so very human that it was painful, and startled the imagination for the moment with the idea that Pythagoras was indeed correct, and that the souls of former men were imprisoned in the bodies of animals; for it was easy, in contemplating this remarkable dog, to suppose that she was possessed of a hidden intelligence not properly belonging to brute life. And yet Juno was only one of the many intelligent beings so frequently to be met with among the dogs, who, in their humble sphere, teach us lessons of devotion, disinterestedness, and friendship.

India is remarkable for wild dogs, among which is the poor Pariah, an inhabitant of the confines of civilization, and yet is never fairly adopted into human society. This dog, naturally gentle, a British officer relates, was caught by the natives in great numbers, and used to feed a tiger, kept in the garrison for the amusement of visitors. On one occasion, a pariah, instead of yielding to fear, stood on the defensive, and as the tiger approached he siezed him by the upper lip. This continued to be done several days, when the tiger not only ceased his attacks but divided his food with the poor dog, and became his friend, and the two animals occupied the same cage for many years. An old lion, in the Tower of London, conceived a liking for a little dog that accidentally got into his cage, and the two animals became inseparable. It was a source of great amusement to observe the impudence of the little puppy, who would bark at visitors while the old lion would look dignifiedly on, seemingly determined to assist his little friend out of any difficulties his presumption might lead to.

Some years ago, it was not uncommon in

Connecticut to employ dogs as motive-power to light machinery. A Mr. Brill had a pair of dogs which he employed together on a sort of tread-mill. After a while the motion of the machinery was noticed from time to time to be considerably retarded, when the tender would go to the mill to see if the dogs were doing their duty, and every thing appeared to be right. Another and another interruption would occur, and so continued, until the owner began to suspect that his dogs were playing some trick upon him. Accordingly he placed an observer where all the movements of the animals could be seen, and the mystery was thus explained. After the two dogs had wrought together for some time, one of them was seen to step off the tread-mill and seat himself where he could catch the first warning of any approaching foot-step. After he had rested awhile he took his place at the wheel again, and allowed his associate to rest: thus these sagacious creatures continued to bear each other's burdens.

An unfortunate dog, in order to make sport for some fools, had a pan tied to his tail, and was sent off on his travels to a neighboring town. He reached his place of destination perfectly exhausted, and lay down before the steps of a tavern, eyeing most anxiously the horrid annoyance fastened behind him, but unable to move a step farther to rid himself of the torment. Another dog, a Scotch shepherd, laid himself down beside him, and, by a few caresses, gaining the confidence of the afflicted cur, proceeded to gnaw the string by which the noisy appendage was attached to his friend's tail, and with about a quarter of an hour's exertion, severed the cord, and started to his legs, with the pan hanging from the string in his mouth, and after a few joyful capers, departed on his travels in the highest glee at his success.

Some years ago, while traveling up the Mississippi river, in common with other passengers on the steamer we were attracted by the docility and intelligence of a pointer dog. This excellent animal would voluntarily return mislaid books, hats, or other trifles to their owners, and seemed to desire to render himself popular by doing such kindly offices. The trick he performed, however, which created most surprise, was taking notes from gentlemen to their wives in the ladies' cabin. This he would do whenever called upon. The person sending the note, would simply call the dog, and his master would give him the directions what to do, and we believe he never made a mistake. The dog would take the paper in his mouth, go among the lady passengers and hunt around, and finally put the note in the lap of the person for whom it was intended.

The son of Dr. Dwight relates, that his father, the greatest theological writer our country has ever produced, was indebted to a dog for his life, the faithful animal obtruding in his pathway, and compelling his horse to turn out of the road he was traveling. In the morning the Doctor discovered that if he had pursued his journey according to his intent, he would have been dashed down a precipice, where to escape with his life would have been an impossibility.

An English gentleman discovered, one morning, that some miscreant had cut off the ears and tail of a favorite horse. A blood-hound was brought to the stable, which at once detected the scent of the villain, and traced it more than twenty miles. The hound then stopped at a door, whence no power could move him. Being at length admitted, he ran to the top of the house, and, bursting open the door of a garret room, found the object he sought in bed, and would have torn him to pieces, had not the huntsman, who had followed the dog on a fleet horse, rushed to the rescue.

A Miss Childs, a keeper of a tavern in London, quite recently possessed a black and white spaniel which performed tricks almost surpassing belief. This dog could play at games of whist, cribbage, and dominoes. In playing these games the dog was placed behind a screen, and had the cards all arranged before him; over this screen he watched his antagonist, and reached with his mouth the suite required. Out of a pack of cards he would instantly select the best cribbage and whist. On the names of any city, county, or town being placed by printed cards before him, the dog would, without hesitation, fetch the one requested, and at the bidding of any one present, and in the absence of his mistress. He could, by the aid of printed cards, tell how many persons might be in the room, how many hats, or the number of coins any one might throw on the floor. After being taken out of the room, if any one present touched a card, the dog on his return would designate it. So numerous, indeed, were the evidences of intelligence exhibited by this dog, that it was impossible to resist the impression that he was possessed of reason.

The following anecdotes of an astonishing dog called "Dandie," are related by Captain Brown:—

"Mr. M'Intyre, patent-mangle manufacturer, Regent Bridge, Edinburgh, has a dog of the Newfoundland breed, crossed with some other, named Dandie, whose sagacious qualifications are truly astonishing, and almost incredible. "When Mr. M'Intyre is in company, how numerous soever it may be, if he but say to the dog, "Dandie, bring me my hat," he immediately picks out the hat from all the others, and puts it in his master's hand. "Should every gentleman in company throw a penknife on the floor, the dog, when commanded, will select his master's knife from the heap, and bring it to him. A pack of cards being scattered in the room, if his master has previously selected one of them, the dog will find it out and bring it to him. A comb was hid on the top of a mantle-piece in the room, and the dog required to bring it, which he almost immediately did, although in the search he found a number of articles, also belonging to his master, purposely strewed around, all which he passed over, and brought the identical comb which he was required to find, fully proving that he is not guided by the sense of smell, but that he perfectly understands whatever is spoken to him. One evening, some gentlemen being in company, one of them accidentally dropped a shilling on the floor, which, after the most careful search, could not be found. Mr. M'Intyre seeing his dog sitting in a corner, and looking as if unconscious of what was passing, said to him, "Dandie, find us the shilling, and you shall have a biscuit." The dog immediately jumped upon the table and laid down the shilling, which he had previously picked up without having been perceived. One time having been left in a room in the house of a lady, he remained quiet for a considerable time; but as no one opened the door, he became impatient, and rang the bell; and when the servant opened the door, she was surprised to find the dog pulling the bell-rope. Since that period, which was the first time he was observed to do it, he pulls the bell whenever he desires; and what appears still more remarkable, if there is no bell-rope in the room, he will examine the table, and if he finds a hand-bell, he takes it in his mouth and rings it. His master, one evening having supped with a friend, on his return home, as it was rather late, he found all the family in bed. He could not find his boot-jack in the place where it usually lay, nor could he find it anywhere in the room after the strictest search. He then said to his dog, "Dandie, I cannot find my bootjack; search for it." The faithful animal, quite sensible of what had been said to him, scratching at the room-door, which his master opened. Dandie proceeded to a very distant part of the house, and soon returned, carrying in his mouth the bootjack, which Mr. M. now recollected to have left that morning under a sofa.

A number of gentlemen, well acquainted with Dandie, are daily in the habit of giving him a penny, which he takes to the baker's shop and purchases bread for himself. One of these gentlemen, who lives in James's Square, when passing some time ago, was accosted by Dandie, in expectation of his usual present. Mr. T—— then said to him, "I have not a penny with me to-day, but I have one at home." Having returned to his house some time after, he heard a noise at the door, which was opened by the servant, when in sprang Dandie to receive his penny. In a frolic Mr. T——gave him a bad one, which he, as usual, carried to the baker, but was refused his bread, as the money was bad. He immediately returned to Mr. T——'s, knocked at the door, and when the servant opened it, laid the penny down at her feet, and walked off, seemingly with the greatest contempt. Although Dandie, in general, makes an immediate purchase of bread with the money he receives, yet the following circumstance clearly demonstrates that he possesses more prudent foresight than many who are reckoned rational beings. One Sunday, when it was very unlikely that he could have received a present of money, Dandie was observed to bring home a loaf. Mr. M'Intyre being somewhat surprised at this, desired the servant to search the room to see if any money could be found. While she was engaged in this task, the dog seemed quite unconcerned till she approached the bed, when he ran to her, and gently drew her back from it. Mr. M. then secured the dog, which kept struggling and growling while the servant went under the bed, where she found 7½*d.* under a bit of cloth; but from that time he never could endure the girl, and was frequently observed to hide his money in a corner of a saw pit, under the dust.

When Mr. M. has company, if he desires the dog to see any one of the gentlemen home, it will walk with him till he reach his home, and then return to his master, how great soever the distance may be. A brother of Mr. M.'s and another gentleman went one day to Newhaven, and took Dandie along with them. After having bathed, they entered a garden in the town; and having taken some refreshment in one of the arbors, they took a walk around the garden, the gentleman leaving his hat and gloves in the place. In the meantime some strangers came into the garden, and went into the arbor which the others had left. Dandie immediately, without being ordered, ran to the place and brought off the hat and gloves, which he presented to the owner. One of the gloves, however, had been left; but it was no sooner mentioned to the dog than he rushed to the place, jumped again into the midst of the company, and brought off the glove in triumph.

A gentleman living with Mr. M'Intyre, going out to supper one evening, locked the garden-gate behind him, and laid the key on the top of the wall, which is about seven feet high. When he returned, expecting to let himself in the same way, to his great surprise the key could not be found, and he was obliged to go round to the front door, which was a considerable distance about. The next morning strict search was made for the key, but still no trace of it could be discovered. At last, perceiving that the dog followed him wherever he went, he said to him, "Dandie, you have the key—go, fetch it." Dandie immediately went into the garden and scratched away the earth from the root of a cabbage, and produced the key, which he himself had undoubtedly hid in that place. If his master places him on a chair, and requests him to sing, he will instantly commence howling, high, or low, as signs are made to him with the finger.

About three years ago a mangle was sent by a cart from the warehouse, Regent Bridge, to Portobello, at which time the dog was not present. Afterwards, Mr. M. went to his own house, North Back of the Canongate, and took Dandie with him, to have the mangle delivered. When he had proceeded a little way the dog ran off, and he lost sight of him. He still walked forward; and in a little time he found the cart in which the mangle was, turned towards Edinburgh, with Dandie holding fast by the reins, and the carter in the greatest perplexity; the man stated that the dog had overtaken him, jumped on his cart, and examined the mangle, and then had seized the reins of the horse and turned him fairly round, and that he would not let go his hold, although he had beaten him with a stick. On Mr. M.'s arrival however, the dog quietly allowed the carter to proceed to his place of destination.

"TAG," a large Newfoundland dog was put to work in a dog power wheel used for churning purposes, but from the first showed a decided dislike for labor. Having been hurt in a fore foot a few months afterwards, he had a rest for a couple of weeks to permit of his foot getting well. When put in the power again he refused to turn it, but held up the foot that had been lame, and howled as if in great pain. His owner supposing that he had perhaps strained the lame foot, let him out, and Tag limped off on three legs, but was soon discovered dashing across a meadow in company with a neighbor's dog, as though he had never been lame. He was called in and again put in the power, and again held up his foot and howled, but a cut or two of the whip convinced him that his trick was seen through, so he went dogfully to work, and nothing of Tag's lameness was afterward seen.

4
14.
21
3
25
11
15
23
6
27
17
7
22
30
9
10
10
29
13
8

MINOS, THE LEARNED DOG.

A very learned man has just written a long article for one of the magazines to prove that dogs, horses and birds have souls. Of course we cannot all agree with him; but we are ready enough to admit that these creatures have minds, —pretty active ones too—whether they have souls or not. Minos, the dog, on page 184, is a wonderful little fellow. He came from Havana, and is now being exhibited in France. His mistress, Madame Hager, has taught him to answer questions which would puzzle some children seven years old. He finds a given number correctly; works out examples in addition, subtraction and division; he can read words that are written and placed before him, and indeed does so many remarkable things that fashionable people in Paris are glad to have him and his mistress visit them at their elegant houses.

Now if a poor dumb dog can learn so much by being simply attentive and obedient, what ought we not to expect of wide-awake boys and girls who can talk, and have not only active minds, but souls as well?

Mr. Youatt gives the following anecdote as a proof of the reasoning power of a Newfoundland dog.

Waiting one day to go through a tall iron gate, from one part of his premises to another, he found a lame puppy lying just within it, so that he could not get in without rolling the poor animal over, and perhaps injuring it. Mr. Youatt stood for awhile hesitating what to do, and at length determined to go round through another gate. A fine Newfoundland dog, however, who had been waiting patiently for his wonted caresses, and perhaps wondering why his master did not get in as usual, looked accidentally down at his lame companion. He comprehended the whole business in a moment—put down his great paw, and as gently and quickly as possible rolled the invalid out of the way, and then drew himself back in order to leave room for the opening of the gate.

We may be inclined to deny reasoning faculties to dogs: but if this was not reason, it may be difficult to define what else it could be.

Mr. Youatt also says, that his own experience furnishes him with an instance of the memory and gratitude of a Newfoundland dog, who was greatly attached to him. He says, as it became inconvenient to him to keep the dog, he gave him to one who he knew would treat him kindly. Four years passed, and he had not seen him; when one day as he was walking towards Kingston, he met Carlo and his master. The dog recollected Mr. Youatt in a moment, and they made much of each other. His master, after a little chat, proceeded towards Wandsworth, and Carlo, as in duty bound, followed him. Mr. Youatt had not, however, got half-way down the hill when the dog was again at his side, lowly but deeply growling, and every hair bristling. On looking about, he saw two ill-looking fellows making their way through the bushes, which occupied the angular space between Rockhampton and Wandsworth roads. Their intention was scarcely questionable, and, indeed, a week or two before, he had narrowly escaped from two miscreants like them. "I can scarcely say," proceeds Mr. Youatt, "what I felt; for presently one of the scoundrels emerged from the bushes, not twenty yards from me; but he no sooner saw my companion, and heard his growling, the loudness and depth of which were fearfully increasing, than he retreated, and I saw no more of him or his associate. My gallant defender accompanied me to the direction-post at the bottom of the hill, and there, with many a mutual and honest greeting, we parted, and he bounded away to overtake his rightful owner. We never met again; but I need not say that I often thought of him with admiration and gratitude."

Newfoundland dogs may readily be taught to rescue drowning persons In France, this forms a part of their education, and they are now kept in readiness on the banks of the Seine, where they form a sort of Humane Society Corps. By throwing the stuffed figure of a man into a river, and requiring the dog to fetch it out, he is soon taught to do so when necessary, and thus he is able to rescue drowning persons. This hint might not be thrown away on our own excellent Humane Society.

The Newfoundland dog may be broken into any kind of shooting, and, without additional instruction, is generally under such command, that he may be safely kept in, if required to be taken out with pointers. For finding wounded game of every description there is not his equal in the canine race, and he is a *sine qua non* in the general pursuit of wild-fowl. These dogs should be treated gently, and much encouraged when required to do anything, as their faults are easily checked. If used roughly, they are apt to turn sulky. They will also recollect and avenge an injury. A traveller on horseback, in passing through a small village in Cumberland, observed a Newfoundland dog reposing by the side of the road, and from mere wantonness, gave him a blow with his whip. The animal made a violent rush at and pursued him a considerable distance. Having to proceed through the same place the next journey, which was about twelve months afterwards, and while in the act of leading his horse, the dog no doubt recollecting his former assailant, instantly seized him by the boot, and bit his leg. Some persons, however, coming up, rescued him from further injury.

A gentleman who had a country house near London, discovered on arriving at it one day that he had brought away a key, which would be wanted by his family in town. Having an intelligent Newfoundland dog, which had been accustomed to carry things, he sent him back with it. While passing with the key, the animal was attacked by a butcher's dog, against which he made no resistance, but got away from him. After safely delivering the key, he returned to rejoin his master, but stopped in the way at the butcher's shop, whose dog again sallied forth. The Newfoundland this time attacked him with fury, which nothing but revenge could have inspired, nor did he quit the aggressor till he had killed him.

A gentleman in Ireland had a remarkable fine and intelligent Newfoundland dog, named Boatswain, whose acts were the constant theme of admiration. On one occasion, an aged lady who resided in the house, and the mother-in-law of the owner of the dog, was indisposed and confined to her bed. The old lady was tired of chickens and other productions of the farmyard, and a consultation was held in her room as to what could be procured to please her fancy for dinner. Various things were mentioned and declined, in the midst of which Boatswain, who was greatly attached to the old lady, entered the room with a young rabbit in his mouth, which he laid at the foot of the bed, wagging his tail with great exultation. It is not meant to infer that the dog knew anything of the difficulty of finding a dinner to the lady's taste, but seeing her distressed in mind and body, it is not improbable that he had brought his offering in the hopes of pleasing her.

On another occasion, his master found this

dog early one summer's morning keeping watch over an unfortunate countryman, who was standing with his back to a wall in the rear of the premises, pale with terror. He was a simple, honest creature, living in the neighborhood. Having to attend some fair or market, about four o'clock in the morning, he made a short cut through the grounds, which were under the protection of Boatswain, who drove the intruder to the wall, and kept him there, showing his teeth, and giving a growl whenever he offered to stir from the spot. In this way he was kept a prisoner till the owner of the faithful animal released him.

A gentleman had a shepherd dog, which was generally kept in a yard by the side of his house in the country. One day a beggar made his way into the yard, armed with a stout stick, with which he defended himself from the attacks of the dog. who barked at and attempted to bite him. On the appearance of a servant the dog ceased barking, and watching his opportunity, he got behind the beggar, snatched the stick from his hand, and carried it into the road, where he left it.

BRAVE DUKE, THE MASTIFF.

The picture on the opposite page portrays the scene of an attempted murder in the Pyrenees, of a young Englishman, by a relative, who was next of kin, and would, by the young man's death, become heir to a vast estate. While making a tour of the continent, the young man was joined by this treacherous relative, who murderously knocked him from a cliff, into a snow-choked chasm, many feet beneath. The snow that was expected to form his winding sheet, and forever conceal his corpse, and the heinous crime committed upon him, from mortal eye, was a cushion to shield him from being dashed to atoms, and his faithful dog "Duke," penetrated the snow till he found him, and then went for assistance, which he conducted to the spot by his signs of distress. The mercenary relative, to save himself from his dastardly deed ended his life by his own hand.

Mr. Millar, a Scotch gentleman, a resident of Melbourne, Australia, entertained the opinion that dogs of ordinary sagacity were capable of recognizing the members of a family which they had not previously seen. He claimed they could do it from resemblance, and also by the scent, which must be similar in families. He had an opportunity of proving very conclusively, both of these theories. The incident was related to us by one of the participants, a lady, now residing in Brooklyn:

While traveling near Melbourne, Mr. Millar was followed home by a young Retriever. Finding him to be a valuable dog, he advertised for the owner, but failing to find one, "Jennie" was installed as the household pet and guardian. Two small children were always accompanied in their walks by her, and no stranger could as much as lay a hand on them. A side gate, near which was her kennel, was guarded against strangers, with the greatest fierceness. At the time of Jennie's installation Miss Lucy, a daughter of fifteen, was away at school, Millar considered her return home would afford a good opportunity to test his theory. "Jennie" had in her kennel, near the guarded gate, a litter of young pups, and was uncommonly savage, but

Mr. Millar did not hesitate to send his daughter alone to the lane and through the gate, which she had barely passed, before the dog came at her in full speed, and with such savageness that her stout heart quailed. When within a few paces from her, the dog stopped, looked in Miss Lucy's face, then approached her and smelt of her dress, making a circuit around her, after which she placed her nose into the young ladie's hand, exhibiting great satisfaction at making her acquaintance.

BEGORRAH.

BEGORRAH.

We give the engraving of the setter "Begorrah," as one of our specimens of the Irish-American Setter. He is a strong, well built setter, with an intelligent head, possessing remarkable strong loins, and is rather more deeply feathered than is represented in the engraving. His color is of a deep red, with white on his breast and toes. He was bred by Mr. Nicholas Saltus of Brooklyn, and is the property of Mr. P. Noël of New York. Begorrah was very highly commended at the New York bench show, this being the first show at which he was exhibited. He was born in 1876; he is a young dog, but promises much. His sire, the celebrated dog "Plunket," is the winner of 11 prizes won at bench shows and field trials. His grand sires, Macdonas' Grouse and Saltus' Dash, are both prize winners; his great grand sires, on his sire side, Hutchingson Bob and Birtwhistle Tim, are celebrated English prize winners. And no doubt Begorrah, if his owner will give him a chance, will not disgrace his ancestors. We wish him the greatest success.

DISEASES OF DOGS.

FEET,—SORE.—When dogs get their feet sore from travelling, it is common to wash them with brine; but which is an erroneous practice. It is better to bathe them with greasy pot-liquor, milk, or buttermilk, and afterwards to defend them from stones and dirt, by wrapping them up. When the feet become sore from any diseased affection of the *claws*, the proper treatment may be seen under that head.

FEVER.—Simple fever seldom, if ever, exists in dogs. Inflammations of the principal organs of the body, as of the lungs, intestines, kidnies, bladder, &c., are very common: but pure fever does not occur, except of the specific kind, as the fever of distemper, and the fever of rabies, &c. &c.

PILES.–Dogs are subject to piles, but the symptoms, by which the complaint shows itself, are by no means known as such, although they are not very dissimilar to the human hæmorrhoids. Piles are brought on by confinement, heat, and heating food; and show themselves by a sore red protruded anus, which the dog aggravates by dragging it on the floor.

Piles are frequently the effect of costiveness. Diarrhœa will also often occasion tenesmus, which may readily be mistaken for piles, the anus appearing red and sore. In such a case, to effect a cure the looseness must be restrained, and the sore anus may be anointed with the ointment directed below, omitting the tar.

The habitual piles will be greatly relieved by the use of the following ointment:—

Take sugar of lead	6 grains.
Tar	half a dram.
Elder ointment, or fine lard	3 drams.

Mix, and anoint the fundament with it two or three times a-day. To keep down the habit towards the disease, feed moderately on cooling food, exercise sufficiently, and, as long as the disposition to it is considerable, give daily one of the following powders:—

Nitre, powdered	half a dram.
Milk of sulphur	3 drams.

Divide into nine, twelve, or fifteen doses.

FLEAS IN DOGS.

Among the numerous inconveniences to which these valuable animals are liable, I hardly know one more troublesome to themselves, or vexatious to their owners, than this common one of fleas. It is, therefore, a very frequent inquiry made, how they can be destroyed, or how they can be prevented from accumulating? Washing the body well with soap-suds, and directly afterwards carefully combing with a small-toothed comb, are the most ready means of dislodging these nimble gentry. But it must be remembered, that the previous washing is only to enable the comb more readily to overtake them: the water does not destroy them; for dogs, who swim every day, still have fleas. These animals are hardy, and soon recover this temporary drowning; the comb, therefore, is principally to be depended on for their caption before they recover. But as washing is not, in many instances, a salutary practice, and in many others is a very inconvenient one, so it becomes a matter of considerable moment to prevent their accumulation without these means.

Innumerable other means I have tried to *drive away* fleas, but the only tolerably certain one I have discovered, is to make dogs sleep on fresh deal shavings. These shavings may be made so fine as to be as soft as a down bed; and, if changed every week or fortnight, are the most cleanly and wholesome one that a dog can sleep on. But, where this is absolutely impracticable, then rub or dredge the dog's hide, once or twice a week, with very finely powdered rosin; if simply rubbed, add some bran. Fleas are not only troublesome, but, by the irritation they occasion, they produce a tendency to mange.

The reader is referred to the advertisement on page 408, for remedies for various ills with which dogs are afflicted.

CASTRATION.

It now and then becomes prudent to perform this operation, from disease of the spermatic chord, or from swellings in the testicles themselves. Whenever such a necessity occurs, although it is not a dangerous operation, it requires the assistance of a veterinary, or a human surgeon. Each testicle should be taken out of the scrotum separately, and a ligature applied, moderately tight only, around the spermatic chord, previous to the separation by means of a scalpel or knife.

In performing this operation on cats, nothing more is requisite, than to make a slight opening on each side the scrotum, to slip out the two testicles, and draw them with the fingers. The rupture of the spermatic chord prevents hæmorrhage, and no future inconvenience is felt. It is often found difficult to secure a cat for this operation; but it may be easily managed in two ways. One is, by putting the head and forequarters of the animal into a boot; the other is managed by rolling her whole body lengthways in several yards of towelling.

FITS.

The fits that usually appear in dogs, though not very different in appearance from each other, arise from very different causes, and, therefore, require very different treatment. The epileptic fits that attack dogs of all ages, and and otherwise apparently healthy, may be idiopathic, or they may probably arise from costiveness or worms, &c. In countries where there are lead mines, dogs have often violent fits from the effects of the lead on the water. The oxen, sheep, goats and horses, of such situations, also participate. Mercury appears to form the best antidote for these contractions, either rubbed externally or given internally.

In the treatment of fits, it is evident that the cause producing them must be attended to, to effect a cure. The immediate fit itself may be removed at once usually, by plunging the dog into cold water; or sprinkling it in his face even, is sufficient in many cases. Whenever a fit has happened to a healthy dog, he should immediately have a brisk purge given him, for fits are very frequently brought on by simple costiveness: and even if such was not the case previous to the fit, this treatment would be the most proper. Should it be at all suspected that the affection arose from worms, treat as directed under that head. Some dogs are so irritable, that whatever raises any strong passion in their minds produces an epileptic attack: hence dogs much confined, on being suffered to run out, frequently have a fit. It is this irritability in the mind, likewise, that produces fits in pointers and setters when hunting; for they are more frequent in the highbred and eager, than in the cool coarse dog. As a general rule, more frequent exercise should be allowed; and, in this latter instance of sporting dogs, the general constitution should as much as possible be strengthened; for fits are here the effect of too much energy of the mind, beyond the powers of the body: and in all cases they are, probably, the effect of a peculiar debility. The irritability of the mind itself should also be attempted to be lessened: in sporting dogs, it is best done by habituating them to the sight of much game, which greatly lessens their eagerness. For a very valuable dog, belonging to a gentleman in Kent, affected with fits whenever he hunted, I recommended a removal into a country more plentifully supplied with game than his neighborhood afforded; the consequence of which was, that though, for a few days after his removal, he had more frequent fits than ever, yet they gradually lessened, and at length wholly left him. Some dogs, however, who exercise much, have fits merely from the repletion of the head: in this case bleeding, an occasional purgative, with a seton worn some time in the neck, proves useful: and, whenever fits have become habitual, a seton should be applied, and kept in some months. Fear in irritable dogs produces fits, of which I have seen innumerable instances.

A very distressing and dangerous kind of epileptic fits sometimes attacks bitches while suckling. In these cases it arises from the owners being too anxious to rear several puppies, by which they burthen the mother beyond her powers: the consequence is an attack of convulsions, which too frequently destroys the animal. Teething in puppies will sometimes produce fits; but some sportsmen, aware of this, fall into another extreme, and consider all the fits of young dogs to originate from this cause: when by far the greater number of these attacks are the effect of worms, or the precursors of distemper.

The fits that are the consequence of distemper, may be usually discovered by the other attendant symptoms: sometimes, however, a fit is the very first symptom, in which case it is remarkable, that the fit augurs nothing unfavourable: but when a fit comes on some time after distemper has made its appearance, the animal seldom recovers. The convulsions accompanying distemper are more frequent in winter than in summer, which shows that warmth is one of the best preventives against these attacks. The convulsion most usually present in distemper begin in the head, and first attacks the muscles of the face and jaws, producing a quick champing of the mouth, with a flow of frothy saliva from the jaws: each succeeding fit is usually stronger and more violent. Another form in which these fits make their appearance in this disease, is, by a running round, with other violent contortions of the whole body. In other instances, there is universal and continued spasm of the whole of the external muscles, very much resembling St. Vitus's dance. All these varieties are sometimes blended, or degenerate into each other.

The idiopathic epilepsy, or those fits which appear habitual, and not dependent on any temporary cause, as costiveness, distemper, &c., are, in general, very difficult of cure. In dogs of very full habit, bleeding, emetics, and an occasional purge, should all be premised. In others, the following medicines may be at once proceeded on :—

Calomel..........................12 grains
Powered foxglove.................12 grains
Powered misletoe.................. 2 drams.

Mix, and divide into nine, twelve, or fifteen parcels, according to the size of the dog, and and give one every morning. After these have been fully tried, in case the attacks do not relax, try the following :—

Lunar caustic. finely powdered......2 grains.
Spiders' web, called cobweb....... .5 grains
Conserve of roses

sufficient to make nine, twelve, or fifteen bales, according to the size of the dog; of which give one every morning.

FRACTURES.

The limbs of dogs are very liable to become fractured; but irritability of the constitution is so much less in these animals than in ourselves, that they suffer comparatively but little on these occasions; and the parts soon reinstate themselves, even without assistance, though in such cases the limb in general remains crooked. The thigh is a very common subject of fracture; and though it appears a most serious bone to break, yet it is one that, with a little assistance, commonly unites straight, and forms a good limb. When a fracture has happened to the *thigh*, in case the violence has injured the fleshy parts also, so as to produce tension, heat, and inflamation, foment with vinegar and water till the swelling is reduced. When this is effected, apply a plaster of pitch or other adhesive matter, spread on moderately firm leather, sufficiently large to cover the outside of the thigh, and to double a little over the inside of it also. Then attach a long splent upon this, which should reach from the toes, to an inch or two above the back, and will steady the limb very much. This splent must be kept in its situation by a long bandage carefully wound round the limb, beginning at the toes, and continuing it up the thigh; when it must be crossed over the back, continued down around the other thigh, and then fastened. This would, however, slip over the tail, without other assistance; for which reason it must be kept in its place by means of another slip passed round the neck and along the back.

Fractures of the *shoulder* should be treated in a similar manner.

In fractures of *fore and hind legs*, very great care is necessary to ensure a straight union. As soon as the inflammation and swelling will admit of it (sometimes there is little or none from the first), apply an adhesive plaster neatly and firmly around the part; then fill up the inequalities by tow or lint, so that the limb shall appear of one size throughout, otherwise the points of the joints will be irritable and made sore by the pressure of the splents. After this has been done, apply two, three, or four, splents of thin pliable wood before, behind, and on each side of the limb, and secure them in their places by flannel bandage. In all fractures, great caution must be observed not to tighten the part, by either the plaster or bandage, so as to bring on swelling; for, when this has been done, mortification has followed. In fractures of the fore-legs, a supporting bandage, with side splents, should be kept on a longer time than is necessary for fractures of the hinder ones. If this precaution is not observed, the leg is apt to become gradually crooked, after the apparatus is removed.

In cases of compound fracture, that is, where there is an open wound, which penetrates to the divided bones: the same means must be pursued as are practised in the human subject. Irritating pointed portions must be sawed off; the loose ones should be removed; and every means must be used to close the wound as early as possible: during which process, the bones should be kept in contact with each other, and supported by soft bandages; until the cicatrization of the wound will allow of proper splents and tighter bandaging.

It likewise not unfrequently happens, that a compound fracture, or even a simple one, when neglected, becomes united by a soft union; that is, instead of the callus interposed between the divided ends being bony, it proves cartilaginous only. In such a case the fractured limb never becomes firm; but, on the contrary, when examined, an obscure motion may be felt, like an imperfect joint, which utterly precludes any strength in the limb. I have frequently been consulted on these cases, all of which originated in the neglect of a proper treatment at first.

As a remedy for the evil, one of two practices must be pursued. We should either open the skin opposite the fracture, and, laying bare the bone, should remove the soft portion interposed, with a fine saw, treating the case afterwards as a compound fracture. Or we should insert a seton exactly through the soft cartilaginous portion, and keep it in ten days or a fortnight. After this time it may be removed, the wound closed, and the part treated as a simple fracture. Either of these plans will usually prove successful, and firmly consolidate the limb; but, when there is no lapping over of the ends of the bones, the latter is the most mild and convenient, and equally certain of success.

AGE OF DOGS.

Dogs do not, as horses, present any exact criterion of their age; nevertheless, attention to the following points will materially assist us in determining the matter.

At about four years, the front teeth lose their points, and each of them preasnts a flattened surface, which increases as the age advances; they likewise become less white, and more uneven. The front teeth suffer earlier than the others, and in dogs fed much on bones, or in those who fetch and carry, as it is called, they are very commonly broken out, while the dog is yet young. The holders, or tushes, are also blunted by the same causes. At seven or eight, the hair about the eyes becomes slightly grey. Gradually, likewise, a greyish tint extends over the face; but it is not till ten, eleven, or twelve years, that the eyes lose their lustre: when they become dim, the dog generally breaks fast, though some last fifteen, sixteen, or seventeen years; and I have seen a mother and son vigorous at twenty and twenty one years old. Such instances as the latter must, however, be considered as rare.

In his native state, perhaps, the dog seldom attains to more than fifteen or sixteen years, while such as live in confinement and luxury, according to the degree of their artificial habits, become old at twelve or thirteen. Now and then an extraordinary exception occurs: the oldest I ever knew had reached his twenty-fourth year, and, at the time I saw him, was still vigorous and lively, and neither lame, nor blind, nor deaf. I am not aware that much difference exists between the various breeds, as to the age they arrive at. Spaniels I, however, think rather long-lived; while terriers, on the contrary, I have seldom observed very old.

Gravel.—Dogs have stone it is certain; that they therefore have gravel also, it is natural to suppose, though it is not always easy to detect it. I have, however, seen the complaint sufficiently well marked. From ten to twenty drops of oil of turpentine, or twice the quantity of spirits of nitre, twice a day, with a few drops of laudanum added to either in case of much pain, will form the best means of relief.

Husk.—This is the popular term in some countries for distemper; it is also in some others the common name for any cough a dog may have. In Ireland it very commonly implies distemper.

Warts in Dogs.—It is not uncommon for dogs to be troubled with warts on some parts of the body; the most frequent of which are the lips, the penis, and the prepuce. These excrecences may be either cut off, or, when they exist in clusters, they may be sprinkled with equal parts of crude sal ammoniac and powdered savine; which commonly effects their removal.

PULSE.

From the greater irritability of lesser animals, and the extreme quickness of their circulation, the motions of the heart and arteries, do not present such exact criteria of health and disease, as they do in the horse and other large animals. In cases of very great affection, the action of the heart, and the pulsations of the larger arteries, may, however, be felt with propriety, and will serve as some guide to ascertain the degree of disease. The pulsations will not only be increased in quickness, but will present a vibratory feel in violent inflammatory affections. In inflammations of the lungs they will be very quick and small, but will increase in fulness as the blood flows during bleeding. Something like the same will occur, but not in an equal degree, in inflammations of the stomach and bowels also. As the pulsatory motions, therefore, are not so distinct in the dog as they are in larger animals; so, in general, the state of the breathing, which, in most cases, is regulated by the circulation, may be principally attended to as a mark of greater or less inflammatory action. When a dog, therefore, pants violently, his circulation, or in other words his pulse, may be considered as quickened.

HYDROPHOBIA—THE SPITZ.

This is the most important subject at present before the public, and is discussed pro and con by both the learned and unlearned. There are many deaths charged to the bite of the Spitz, who is accused of being a snappish dog, and over fond of using his teeth. But the Spitz has his friends, and will not be made a scape-goat-of for all the other dogs. Fortunately for him, most of the recent cases of hydrophobia have been caused by the bite of dogs of another species. His enemies retort, that this does not clear the Spitz from being the cause, as the cur may have been inoculated with the poison, by the bite of a Spitz.

Ex-Surgeon General of the Army, Dr. Wm. A. Hammond, who is regarded as one of the most eminent authorities on nervous diseases in this country, gives his views on hydrophobia, which is now conceded to be a nervous disease. The Doctor concurs in the dangerous nature of the Spitz dog, and considers theory of the harmlessness of the Spitz absurd.

He says Spitz dogs are more prone to excite hydrophobia in the human system than any other breed of dogs he knows of, and pronounces the Spitz a cross between the Pommeranian hound and the Arctic fox. All hybrids are bad. While the blending of varieties is good, that of genera is accompanied with evil results. The disease can only be communicated by the saliva or by a wound, and not by the injection of the blood of the hydrophobic animal. The saliva is the only poisonous part of animals. The saliva of the rattlesnake will kill you, and yet you can eat the rattlesnake.

Until more comprehensive investigation settles the question, we are justified in assuming from our present experience that the saliva of the Spitz dog is more uniformly poisonous than that of any other dog, and experience teaches that the saliva of a dog not suffering from rabies may be poisonous under certain conditions—when the dog is in a state of anger or fury or merely in a condition of excitement.

Dr. Hammond says the Spitz is absolutely of

no use, and in a matter involving precious lives, it is better to be on the safe side. Nothing would be lost by exterminating the Spitz.

A dog perfectly healthy, says Dr. Hammond, or at least free from rabies, may produce the disease by his bite through his saliva. In the case of McCormick the dog was exhibited to the Neurological Society more than a month after the bite, and as hydrophobia runs its course in seven or eight days, and as the dog invariably dies, he either could not have had it or he could not have been the dog in question: remember, it takes a wound to produce death. You might swallow the saliva and it would not kill you unless you had, perhaps, an abrasion on your lip. The saliva is only poisonous when communicated through a wound. You get lockjaw, or tetanus, from a simple wound, and hydrophobia seems to be tetanus plus a group of other symptoms.

We can recognize the origin and symptoms of hydrophobia as we can those of scarlet fever or measles. To this day no one has discovered the primal origin of scarlet fever. We know that we cannot cure hydrophobia. Remember that there never has been a cure on record. It is necessary not to confound the prevention with the cure. There are a great many people who claim to have invented cures for hydrophobia, but they mean cures after the bite and before the poison has been developed. This is an easy matter, but no cure has as yet been effected after the poison (which lies dormant in the system a few weeks, and sometimes even several months, and even several years) has been developed. In the early part of last fall a distinguished officer of the army came to me, who had been bitten by a dog, manifestly hydrophobic. I cauterized the wound with a red hot iron, and I regard him as perfectly safe.

Dr. Hammond seems to be well sustained in his assertion that there is no cure for hydrophobia after it has permeated the system, but prevention is tried with a great deal of faith. Nevertheless in almost every case of hydrophobia that has occurred of late, the parts bitten had been cauterized. But whether with hot iron, as Dr. Hammond recommends, or with caustic, we are unable to say. Any other preventative will be eagerly sought after by the public. Dr. Blaine, (formerly Blaine & Youatt, the celebrated Veterinary Surgeons,) recommended excising the wound. Immediate excision or cauterization was not considered absolutely necessary, although the sooner the better. Dr. Blaine also used an internal remedy, in which he had great faith, having administered it several hundred times, with less than a dozen failures of immunity. In all cases of failure, the bites were on the head.

Where a human life was at stake, he also cut out the bitten part, unless the patient strongly objected to the severe treatment Below will be found the formula for Dr. Blaine's preventative.

"Take of the fresh leaves of the Tree Box, 2 ounces, fresh leaves of Rue, 2 ounces, Sage half an ounce, chop finely, boil in pint of water till reduced to half a pint; strain and press out the liquor. Beat in a mortar, or otherwise thoroughly bruise, and boil in pint of new milk, to half a pint. which press out as before. Both fluids to be mixed, and divided into three doses, and taken, one every morning on a empty stomach. Double this quantity would be required for a horse; one third for a small dog, and half to two thirds for a large one, or other small animals. It is undoubtedly a hard dose to take and retain, and would never become "popular," unless there was unbounded faith that it was the only remedy against the dreaded and fatal disease.

Some years since, it was stated that steam bath was a remedy for hydrophobia, and had been used with success. But, like many other remedies, it was found not to be infallible. It is again recommended with great confidence, as an auxiliary in preventing and curing. Hydrophobia, it is said by some, is located in the stomach, and the treatment should be that which has a tendency to throw the foul matter from it. A course of Thomsonion treatment is recommended for this. No. 6 and skullcap, steeped in milk, and in cases where symptoms of hydrophobia are shown, and fluids can not be administered, enemas of lobelia and valerian are to be administered, which will cause the foul matter to be thrown from the stomach, relax the muscles and relieve from spasms. This treatment, with steam baths, must be followed for several weeks. For a week or two daily, and two or three times a week afterwards.

Only experience can prove the efficacy of this as a remedy. But, as the most skilled physicians make no pretensions to a remedy when once attacked, and only cauterization as a preventative, nothing is risked in resorting to this course of treatment possibly it may lead to happy results.

It is well to always avoid dogs or cats, which act strangely, or endeavor to conceal themself in dark or secluded corners. That is a sign of illness in almost every species of the brute creature. Guarding against bites of the Spitz and diseased dogs of all descriptions, is certainly the best preventative.

THE REV. MR. MACDONNA, WITH HIS DOG "MUNGO."

QUEEN VICTORIA'S DEER-HOUNDS,

JOHN MATTHEWS'S "DUKE,"

THE GREAT BENCH SHOW

Was held in the Hippodrome, which had been fitted up expressly for the purpose. Stalls were erected around the capacious arena for the accommodation of the dogs; but the entries were so much in excess of the calculations that extra stalls were built, at the last moment, inside the arena. There were also two rings into which the several classes of dogs were taken to be judged.

The show opened Tuesday, May 8th. As early as ten o'clock Monday the dogs began to arrive. They came by all sorts of conveyances. Some were packed in huge coops marked "with care," others were led by stout iron chains, and still others were carried in baskets or in the arms of their owners. Among those bringing their pets for exhibition were many elegantly dressed ladies. Crowds of men and boys surrounded the entrance. Some of the dogs were disposed to be quarrelsome, especially the big fellows, and many times the crowd scattered with ludicrous haste at the unexpected growl of some ferocious-looking brute. There was danger from some of them, too, for their owners took great care to keep them at a safe distance from the legs of imprudent bystanders. Not a few had great difficulty in holding the powerful animals in. Other dogs were quiet and friendly, but not less annoying to their masters by plunging about and entangling their chains in seemingly inextricable confusion.

The spectacle inside the arena, when every thing was in readiness, was very attractive. There were over eleven hundred entries of all classes, from the huge Siberian blood-hound, the magnificent St. Bernard dog, the Newfoundland and the mastiff, down to the most delicate toy dogs. To the latter were devoted several stands in the centre of the arena, and this was one of the most attractive spots in the show. The little things were rigged up with ribbons, mats, cushions, bells, and lace collars, in the most dainty style. Two large pups with lace collars were very amusing. Others were the occupants of a number of mahogany-framed glass cases. One of these, a tiny mite of a thing, with long silken hair, bore the ferocious name of "Danger." There were also three beautiful Italian greyhound puppies, five delicate Japanese puppies, and six little white balls nestling under their Blenheim spaniel mother.

The principal attendance was during the evenings, when the building was crowded to its full capacity. There were quite as many ladies as gentlemen present, and they seemed to take quite as much interest in the dogs. The only drawback to the enjoyment of the show was the dreadful howling that filled the building and at times almost prevented conversation. Mr. BERGH's speech on Tuesday evening was inaudible six feet from where he stood. The larger dogs were, as a rule, dignified and quiet; but the petted darlings of the drawing-room expressed their anguish over their imprisonment and loss of home luxuries in tones that must have pierced the very hearts of their fair owners.

The show was in every sense a great success, and will probably prove to be the first of a long series of such exhibitions. It was held under the auspices of the Westminster Kennel Club, and for a first enterprise of the kind, the management was noticeably free from annoyances and mistakes. It lasted four days, and every one who visited it was delighted and entertained. But if the question of holding another bench show were left to the dogs, it would doubtless be rejected by a large majority.

MR. JONES'S SIBERIAN BLOODHOUND "BRUNO."

THE BONES OF THE CANINE SKELETON.

The first portion of the skeleton which claims our attention is the skull. The shape of this extremity is familiar to every one, and differs in the various breeds, being more elongated in the greyhound, for instance, than in the Bulldog or Newfoundland, where it forms a well-rounded dome, with a wide cranial cavity, or brain-pan. All that it is necessary for the reader to note is —

The *General Configuration of the Skull* and its different shapes according to breed, bearing in mind that nearly all the breeds are well developed as regards brain-pan.

The *Nasal Bone*, well developed in the dog.

The *Occipital Bone*, also well developed. This portion of the dog's head is called the occiput.

The *Orbital Cavity of the Eye.*

The *Superior Maxilla*, or upper jaw.

The *Inferior Maxilla*, or lower jaw. The teeth of the two jaws in the majority of breeds ought to meet evenly in front; in other breeds, as the Bull, the King Charles', &c., the under jaw projects more or less.

The *Teeth.* — Unlike the cat, who has to be content with thirty teeth, the dog is liberally supplied with these useful weapons, having, when full-grown, forty-two — viz., 12 incisors, 4 canine or tusks, and 26 molars; 20 teeth in the upper, and 22 in the lower jaw.

Dogs begin to get their first or milk teeth at a month old, and the permanent teeth ought to be all perfect when the animal is six and a half months old.

The *Temporal Bone*, more prominent in some dogs than in others.

We next come to the Vertebral Column. This column or spine is designed by Nature for the protection of the nervous spinal column, a continuation of the brain matter.

From this column nerves escape by foramina through the vertebræ, to be distributed to all the various organs, muscles, and bones of the body. The vertebral column is also a support to the limbs and the whole osseous system. The spine is composed of small round perforated bones called vertebræ, beautifully hinged together. They are divided into—

The *Seven Cervical Vertebræ*, corresponding to the neck of the animal.

The *Thirteen Dorsal Vertebræ*—the back.

The *Seven Lumbar Vertebræ*—the loin.

The *Three Sacral Vertebræ*, forming a portion of the pelvis, and

The *Caudal Vertebræ*, forming the bones of the tail, or stern, and numbering (if left alone) from 16 to 21.

The *os innominatum* is the principal bone of the pelvis. Hinged to this by a ball and socket joint is

The *Femur*—the thigh-bone—a long, sturdy, and strong bone, jointed by its lower extremity to three bones, namely—

The *Patella*, or knee-pan; and

The *Tibia*, which gives its chief support to the patella, and is the principal bone of the leg or hock, is, like the femur, a long, strong bone, but differently shaped. The other bone of the leg is

The *Fibula*, a much more slender bone, situated on the outer portion of the tibia, and joined to that bone by a strong fibrous tissue.

The *Bones of the Hock Joint.*

The *Foot Proper*, commencing at the hock joint, comprises the *calcaneus* or heel-bone—the *astragalus*, the *schaphoid*, three cuneiform bones; five metatarsal bones—the longest bones in the foot (one of these metatarsals is only rudimentary); and the first, second, and third phalanges, ending in the nails.

The ribs of the dog are in number thirteen at each side. They are articulated to the vertebræ above and partly to the *sternum*, or to each other beneath. The ribs of nearly all classes of well-bred dogs ought to be well sprung.

The *Sternum*, or breast-bone, is a flattish or scimitar-shaped bone, composed of several pieces joined together, and lying underneath the ribs, at the lower portion of the chest. It needs little further description here.

The shoulder in the dog is composed of two bones, the *Clavicle* and the *Scapula*. The former of these barely needs mention, so unimportant and rudimentary is it.

The *Scapula* or shoulder-blade is a much more important bone. It is flat, broad, and moderately strong, especially towards its lower portion, where it articulates with the *humerus*. Its shape can be seen from a glance at the illustration. In most dogs, especially sporting dogs, this bone should slope well backwards. On the outer surface a strong bony ridge descends for the attachment of the muscles.

The *Humerus* is the one single bone of the arm. It is a long bone, very strong, and somewhat bent or curved.

The bones of the forearms are two, namely—

The *Radius*, and

The *Ulna*. In the human being the radius is much the stronger bone, and the two lie parallel. In the dog the two bones are about equal in size, the ulna being thicker at its upper portion, and the radius stronger at its lower. Again, the bones are not perfectly parallel, but slightly, or in a very small degree, positioned like a St. Andrew's cross. These two bones are hinged to each other at the upper and lower surfaces.

From the lower portion of these two bones the forefoot proper commences, comprising the following bones, viz.—

Seven carpal bones, corresponding to the human wrist-bones, five metacarpal bones, corresponding to the bones joining the wrist to the fingers in the human subject (the bones that are in the back of the hand), and the five digits or fingers, which in the dog are analogous to those of the human skeleton. Each digit is composed of three columnar bones. Lastly, they are united at their extremities to the nails, which grow therefrom.

THE ONLY ESQUIMAUX IN THE SHOW.

GLOSSARY OF WORDS USED BY THE FANCY.

Apple-headed.—A term used to designate the peculiar roundness of the black-and-tan Toy Terrier. This roundness is considered a point of beauty by some judges.

Beltons (Blue and Lemon).—The spotted or flecked Laverack Setter.

Babbler.—A dog that gives too much tongue when working. Generally applied to those Spaniels which ought to be mute.

Broody.—A broody bitch—one that, from its length and conformation, gives evidence of being a likely mother.

Blood.—A blood—a dog with every appearance of high breeding.

Brisket.—The chest—of a Setter, for instance.

Blaze.—The white line up the face of some breeds, such as the St. Bernard, Scotch Collie, or Blenheim.

Button-ear.—A term used to define the peculiar shape of some Bulldogs' ears.

Braque.—A German name given to a Dahshund of unusual size.

Cat-footed.—Having a foot like a cat—the orthodox foot for Greyhounds and nearly all other dogs.

Cobby.—An expression used in describing some Fox Terriers, with reference to their symmetry and well-knit appearance.

Condition.—A dog's being in condition means that he is in a state of perfect health: just enough flesh, and no more, and his coat in excellent order.

Character.—When a dog shows character, he shows in a marked manner the points of the breed to which he belongs.

Crest.—The upper ridge or portion of a dog's neck. Generally applied to sporting dogs, as the Setter.

Comb Fringe.—The beautiful straight fringe of feather that droops from the tail of a Setter.

Dewlap.—That portion of loose skin that hangs from the throat of some dogs, as the Bloodhound and Bulldog.

Dewclaw.—An extra claw found on the inside of the lower portion of the hind leg of many dogs, especially the St. Bernard, where it is admissible. In the Newfoundland it is not, but it is often seen on the Scotch Collie. It is usually cut off when found in puppies where its presence would not enhance, or would spoil them for show purposes.

Faking.—Interfering with a dog's natural appearance for the sake of hiding defects, as dyeing a Retriever's breast, if white; or pulling the flag, if any, from a curly-coated Retriever's tail. "A Fake" is the deed done.

Flews.—The chaps or hanging lips of a dog, as the Bloodhound.

Frill.—The beautiful half-crescentic mass of feather under a Scotch Collie's throat.

Flag.—A term applied to the drooping feather on some dogs' tails, as that of the flat-coated Retriever.

Feather.—A word used to describe the long hair and locks in a dog's coat, and the coat of long-haired dogs generally.

Fiddle-headed.—A very expressive term, used to define the lantern jaws of some big badly-bred Mastiffs.

Felted.—When the long feather of a Collie or Retriever gets matted into masses that bid defiance to anything short of scissors, it is said to be "felted," a condition which is a disgrace to the dog's owner.

Fixed.—Means astonished. Judges are fixed by some particularly and rarely bred dogs.

Hare-foot.—Synonymous with spoon-foot: defining the shape of foot some dogs have, as the Pug, which has the toes well split up, as in the hare.

Hover. The bed or nest of the otter, generally built of straw or stubble, withered grass, and weeds, in a hollow of bank or rock by the river-side.

Haw.—The reddish portion of the inner eyelid of the dog, shown in the Otterhound, Bloodhound, and St. Bernard.

Kissing-spots.—The spots on the cheeks of some Toys and others: as the mole on the cheek of the Pug.

Landseer.—A name given by the author, and now generally adopted, to the great white-and-black Newfoundland, which the immortal painter so loved to portray.

Lippy.—Applied to hanging lips of some dogs where hanging lips should not exist, as in the Bull Terrier.

Lengthy.—Possessing length of body, as the Newfoundland ought to do. A Skye is long, a Newfoundland or St. Bernard lengthy.

Leather.—The skin. Especially applied to the dog's ear.

Lady Pack.—Hounds are usually hunted in packs all of one sex. The bitches are called the "lady pack."

Level.—A term used to describe some Fox-terriers. A dog's teeth are said to be level when the jaws are neither overhung nor underhung. You cannot put your nail behind a tooth when the mouth is closed.

Leggy.—Having the legs too long in proportion to the body. "Shaped like a milking-stool," (Idstone).

Mane.—The feather which is massed on the shoulders of the Collie and Newfoundland. That on the breast of the Blenheim is also called the "mane," which is quite a subversion of the term.

Massiveness.—A term applied to the body of a good Newfoundland or St. Bernard, and descriptive of the solidity of frame.

Pasterns.—The ankles.

Pig-jawed. Having jaws in the formation of a pig. Applied to Setters when the upper jaw protrudes.

Peaked.—A word used to define the formation of some dogs' craniums, as that of the Bloodhound and Irish Setter.

Piley.—Applied to the coats of some dogs, as the Dandie, signifying that the coat is a mixture of hardish and soft hair.

Pencilled Toes.—The toes of a well-bred black-and-tan Terrier are "pencilled," or marked with black upon the upper or convex portion. A point of beauty.

Pinwire.—Descriptive of the coats of some Terriers.

Quality.—A term difficult to translate. It signifies that mixture of blood and breediness that you see in many good dogs, notably sporting dogs. It is seen in shape, and coat, and eye, and delicacy of form, &c.

Ring-tailed. The word tells its own tale. It is seen in the tails of some Deerhounds.

Rose-ear.—Another form of ear of Bulldog. This ear "folds at the back, and the tip laps over outwards, showing part of the inside," (Idstone).

Stern.—The tail. Mostly used in sporting *parlance*.

Stifle.—The joint next the buttock.

Stocky.—A bitch is called stocky when she looks as if she could throw good pups and be a good mother.

Stop.—The hollow or indentation between the eyes of some breeds, as the Bulldog, the King Charles, &c.

Sting.—A dog's tail is sting-like when it is broad at the

base and tapers to a fine point, as in the well-bred Pointer.

SLUT.—Bitch, or lady-dog. Not often used.

SNIPEY.—A dog's muzzle, when long, narrow, and peaked, is so designated.

SNAPDOG, or WHIPPET.—A kind of small Greyhound, used in some countries for rabbit-coursing.

SCIMITAR, OF SABRE CURVE.—Words used to define the correct carriage in the tail of the Setter.

THROATINESS.—Looseness of the skin of the throat, or dewlap. Quite correct in the Bulldog and Dachshund, for example, but intolerable in the Pointer.

TONGUE.—Equivalent to voice.

TULIP-EAR.—Partly pricked, and drooping at the tip.

THUMB-MARK.—An obliquely-shaped black mark crossing the foot of a well-bred Black-and-tan above the toes.

TIGHT-LIPPED.—Having no flew; as in the fighting Bull-and-terrier Dog.

WEEDY.—A very expressive word, as applied to a dog who looks leggy, thin, badly bred, and apparently going to seed.

RULES AND REGULATIONS

OF THE

WESTMINSTER KENNEL CLUB.

No dog belonging to the Westminster Kennel Club, or to any member thereof, will be entered for premium, although all will be on exhibition.

This Bench Show will be held under the rules adopted by the National American Kennel Club, as

RULE 1. Every person who wishes to exhibit at any show held under these Rules, must at the time of entry clearly identify by name and age (if known) the dog he intends to exhibit, and the name of the sire and dam (if known) must be given. If the name of a dog has been changed it is necessary in entering the said dog to give his old as well as his new name.

RULE 2. If a dog shall be entered without being clearly identified as directed in Rule 1, he shall forfeit any prize that may have been awarded him, and if the omission be detected in time he shall not be allowed to compete, and shall forfeit all entrance fees and subscriptions.

RULE 3. The committee or authorities of any show held under the Kennel Club Rules, may reserve to themselves the right to exclude any dog or dogs belonging to any person who has been proved, to the satisfaction of the committee of the Club, to have misconducted himself, in any way, in connection with dogs, dog-shows or dog-trials.

RULE 4. No dog shall be qualified to compete, or entitled to receive a prize, if awarded, who is suffering from mange, or any other form of contagious disease.

RULE 5. A person, duly qualified, appointed by the committee, shall decide whether a dog is, or is not, suffering from mange or any other contagious disease, and shall give his opinion immediately to the secretary, or committee of the show, in writing, and if found to be afflicted with any such disease, the dog shall be at once removed.

RULE 6. A dog that has been exhibited or has won a prize in a class exclusively for puppies under twelve months old, is not thereby excluded from being exhibited in a class where previous prize winners are not allowed to compete.

RULE 7. All imported dogs and their progeny on both sides (but not the progeny of the latter) shall be entered in the imported class, and be debarred from entering in the native class; but no native dog shall be debarred from entering in the imported class.

RULE 8. Dogs are to be judged by the scale of points used at recent bench shows and copied from the *Fanciers' Gazette.*

In addition to the above, the following Rules and Regulations will be strictly enforced:

1.—All judging will be done in public on a raised stand prepared for the purpose, and collars bearing owners' names will be removed or covered before the dogs are brought before the judges.

2.—An entry fee of $2 will be charged for each animal entered. The entry fee must in all cases accompany the entry. Entries will be received until noon on April 25th, except in case of foreign exhibitors, who will be allowed until May 1st. Dogs must be at the Madison Avenue entrance of the Garden by 8 o'clock on the morning of Tuesday, May 8th, but it is earnestly requested that when possible all dogs will be on hand on Monday, the 7th. The entrance fee will include care and feed of dogs.

3.—It is required that a price be named for each dog at the time of making the entry to be printed in the catalogue, at which price the dog may be claimed; the exhibitor, of course, having the option of naming a prohibitory price. A commission of 10 per cent. will be charged on all sales, and the same must be effected through the Secretary or Superintendent.

4.—All entries must be made on blanks furnished by the Club, which can be had from the Superintendent by addressing him at his office, No. 17 Chatham Street, (P. O. Box 2832.)

5.—The authorities will use due diligence for the care and safety of all dogs exhibited (watchmen being on duty both night and day,) but it must be distinctly understood that they will not be responsible for loss of or damage to any dog exhibited, whether the result of accident or any other cause.

6.—The pedigree of all dogs entered is desired, although not actually required, except in case two dogs in same class should be so nearly equal that judges cannot agree which is the best. In such case if one has an authenticated pedigree and the other has not, the premium will be given to the dog with the pedigree.

7.—The decision of judges will be final in

all cases, unless misrepresentation or collusion can be shown—should this occur the Executive Committee will use their discretion in the matter. Allowance will be made for dogs that have been worked this season, and no deduction will be made for docked tails or ears.

8.—Judges will be instructed to withhold the prizes offered in any class where there is no competition, unless the animal exhibited possesses suitable merit, in which case their discretion shall govern the prize to be awarded, either first or second, and they will then be instructed to withhold prizes where the dogs do not come up to the proper standard of merit.

9.—Exhibitors will be permitted to take home their dogs every evening after the show is closed upon leaving a deposit of Five Dollars with the check clerk and surrendering their entry tickets, both of which will be returned on the re-producing of the dog in the morning before 10 o'clock. If prize winners should be taken out and not returned the prizes will be forfeited.

10.—Exhibitors need not accompany their dogs. They can be sent direct to the exhibition hall, and direction cards, printed for this purpose, will be furnished by the secretary. All dogs will be promptly returned to their owners at the close of the exhibition, or otherwise disposed of as they may direct.

11.—The show will be open from 10 **A. M.** to 10 **P. M.** The judging will be done on the first day, and the ribbons will be attached to the stalls of the winners immediately thereafter.

12.—The prizes, which will be in gold coin for the several classes except Champions, will be presented in public on the evening of May 10th, at 9 P. M

13.—The term dog or bitch implies that the animal is over one year old. The age of it must be computed from the date of birth up to the 8th of May.

14.—*Railway Arrangements.*—Arrangements for the free transportation of dogs are in course of completion with all Railway Companies centering in New York, and will be duly announced.

15.—The members of the Committee will be in constant attention, and especial attention will be given to the care of pet dogs.

16.—Judges will be instructed to give the awards of Highly commended and Commended where in their option it is warranted.

17.—No dog will be received unless supplied with suitable chain and collar. Bitches with pup and small pups weaned, will have suitable pens provided. Toy dogs will be furnished with suitable cages.

18.—Exhibitors residing abroad may ship their dogs to the care of the Westminster Kennel Club. If for sale, certificate from the American Consul at the port of shipment that they are exported for breeding purposes must accompany them. If to be returned, the Club will give a bond to the Custom House authorities.

PRIDE OF

Pedigree of the pure Laverack setter dog, "PRIDE OF THE BORDER," as carefully
Broughall Cottage, Whitchurch, Shropshire, England. Imported in 1874, by his present
ings, and is sire of Mr. Laverack's celebrated Stock and Field Dog, *Blue Prince*; Mr. D
Manchester; Mr. Dicken's *Blue Dash*, and of many other highly valued Setters.

FOX FARM, MORRIS PLAINS, N. J.

E BORDER.

'ected by Mr. Laverack, under date of March 31st, 1875. Bred in 1869, by Mr. Laverack,
ner. Mr. Charles H. Raymond. PRIDE OF THE BORDER is a white dog, with liver mark-
ry Hollin's *Silk* and *Tory*; Mr. Langston's *Blue Peter*, prize winners at Birmingham and

LE 2D............	DASH 2D............
ck, white & tan.)	(blue mottled.)

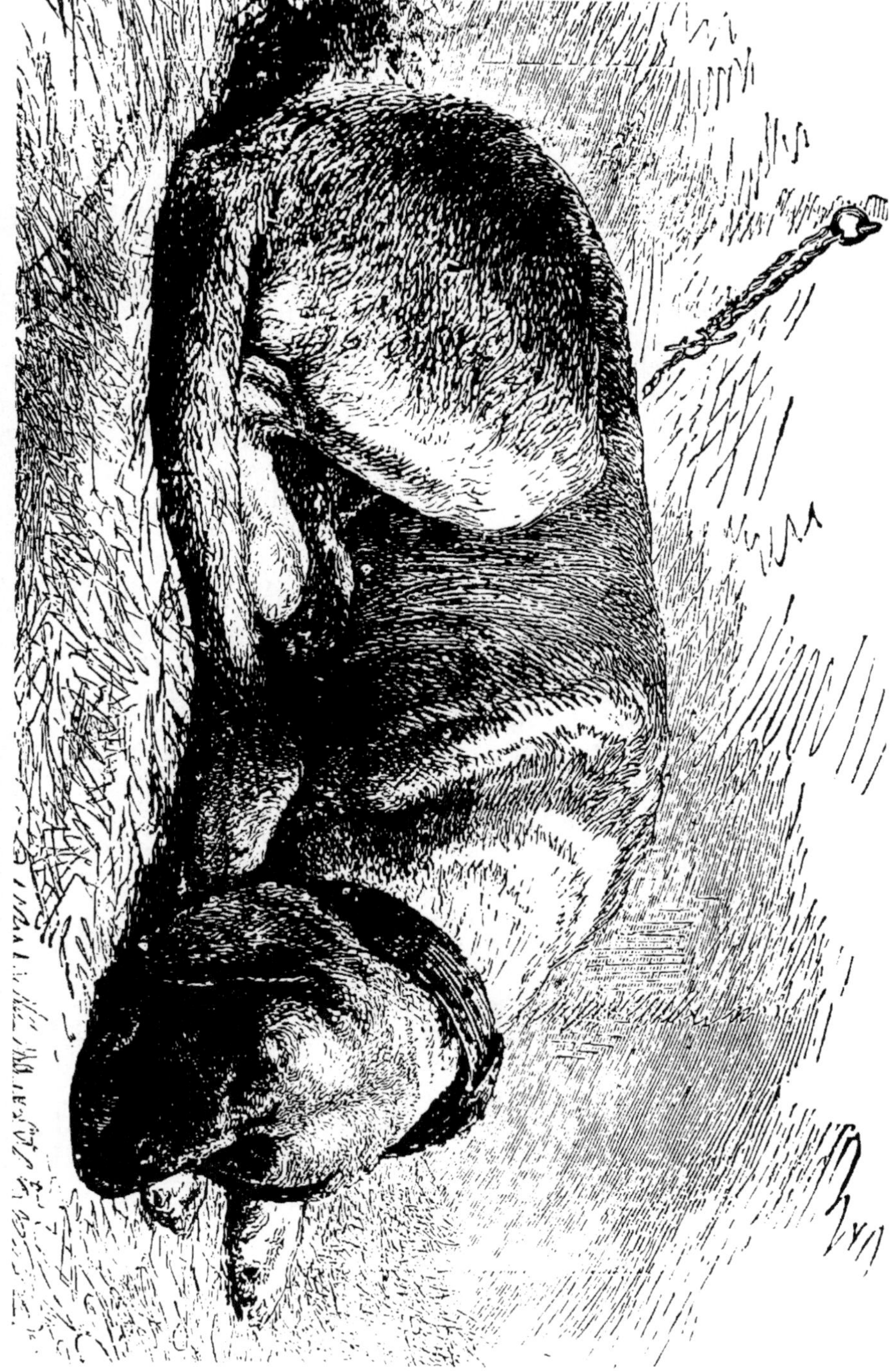

NERO,

THE LARGEST DOG IN EUROPE.

Nero, the subject of the foregoing engraving, was first exhibited at the Crystal Palace Dog Show in 1871, in the open or keepers' class, and was there, without a moment's hesitation, awarded the first prize. He was then about seven years old, and remarkable for his symmetrical proportions, beautiful brown color, and enormous size; of the latter some idea may be formed by stating that at that time he weighed nearly 165 pounds. It is extremely difficult to assign a distinctive name to this breed. Some incline to the belief that it is analogous to the southern hound; by some it is styled Welsh mastiff, and by others a cross with (with what not stated) the English bloodhound. The question of any suspicion of bloodhound is met by the dissimilarity of the ears which in the bloodhound are long, fine, and pendulous; whereas in this dog they are short and a little coarse, and, when excited, are slightly "pricked;" and whereas the bloodhound, as well as the mastiff, is well known to be averse to water, this breed would almost live in it. It is not improbable that it is a descendant of the hounds used in the chase centuries since, when wolves were common in England, the keenness of their scent being very fine.

The dog is the property of Mr. Howel W. Williams, of Swansea, Wales.

BRUNO.
Nunquam Dormio.

Printed in Great Britain
by Amazon